For Noah

Who's Been Talking?

Rony Robinson

And now do yours!

16/8/11

Buy our books online at
www.aldbooks.co.uk

Printed and published by:
ALD Print Limited
279 Sharrow Vale Road
Sheffield S11 8ZF

Telephone 0114 267 9402
E:mail a.lofthouse@btinternet.com

ISBN 978-9-01587-88-3
First published October 2010

A - Z

I've sort of arranged myself A - Z.

That's because just as I was starting to write, I remembered a book from 1969 by this nearly forgotten experimental novelist called B. S. Johnson.

It's the story of a writer who goes back to a North he can't quite remember, and his memories won't come back in quite the right order even when he can.

If I'm remembering it right.

It's called *The Unfortunates,* and comes in loose pages, in a box. You are told to shuffle them up before you start.

The past doesn't come back in the right order.

And it comes back differently each time.

*

When I was researching my last radio play, *49 Letters,* about a man from the Sheffield family history archives whose life had gone a bit random in middle age, I ended up randomly watching the film of *Sleepless in Seattle.*

The famous line from that is -

> *Destiny is something we invented because we can't stand the fact that everything that happens is accidental.*

History is like that, invented. Ours and theirs.

So, pinching as we go (or borrowing from thieves, as someone said) we're off.

I've put in some footnotes because life's like that isn't it?[1]

I've fiddled the A - Z's a bit, and put some things in boxes.

If this isn't a borrowed copy, snap its spine and shuffle its pages if you want. Or just begin at the beginning. It's what I did.[2]

---

1 You only realise some things after.
2 And it's all for charity remember.

1. Doctor Marshall Drank The Whisky

Beginning

One moonlit December night, my Dad was coming home late from the Town Hall and was about to dive into the *Marples* pub in Fitzalan Square.

He loved diving into pubs, though he never drank more than a pint and a half at a time in them.

Anyway, at the last minute on that December moonlit night he decided not to dive, but to go on to Pond Street instead and get the 45 bus home, because he had a bit of a tickle that he thought might be the beginning of pneumonia.

It's a good job he didn't dive.

Anyway, he got home to 6 Laverdene Drive, had his tea, had a nap, read the *Daily Herald,* and went to bed with his tickle.

He was 40, Mum was 33, and Our Geth was 5.

Twelve days later, on Christmas Eve, Nanny Jessop trudged over from Lemont Road, all black in the blackout, and delivered me in the front bedroom, while Dr Marshall sat in the kitchen drinking Dad's Christmas whisky.[3]

When I was born, at 11.56pm, weighing three and three quarter pounds, my bottom was like your first two fingers stuck together, and I was so small they weren't sure if I was a boy or a girl.

And that's the end of the Beginning.

(And nearly the end of my Dad).

---

3 Dad always said he caught a cold that night, too.

Boxing Day

By Boxing Day, Dad's tickle had turned into pneumonia, four years before penicillin, and eight years before the NHS.

Dr Marshall came back, drank the rest of the whisky and ordered him to turn me and my Mum out of the front bedroom bed, and lie there until he died, or didn't.[4]

I'd been conceived in that front bedroom bed on Easter Sunday, March 24th, nine months earlier. Double summertime hadn't started and the blackout was up. The light was off and they were in pyjamas and nighties, because it was still only March even if the first wood anemones were already out in Gilly Woods, and because I never saw my parents naked, winter or summer, in or out of bed, and I'm not going to start now.

Anyway, that is how my wonderful always-loving Mum and Dad made me.

Afterwards they held hands all night, because I was wanted[5], though not by Our Geth who was fast asleep through the wall, full of the last Easter egg before the real War started.

---

4 He did die, and of pneumonia, and in that bed, but not till 44 years later.
5 I don't know what contraception my parents used, though when I was 13 I found a terracotta rubbery bulby thing with a tube, in the bottom left-hand drawer of the dressing table where my Mum kept her Yorkshire netball badge, and the tinted photo of herself at 21. The rubbery bulby thing was never there again, however often I looked.

Brief Lives
Would these have been better titles for this book?

37 For Ever!

Look Where Your Hand Is Now John!

Just Like Me!

What Did Nanny Jessop Say?

The Boy Who Grew Up To Write The Beano!

Where's Rony?

Hark At Me!

Burke's Best

Twenty-Six Years Without A Mistake!

Can You Hear Me Mother?

The Naked Broadcaster

I've Gone Dead!

Brief Lives

Camp Variety

Dad got over his near-death experiences with the *Marples*, pneumonia and me, and went back to the office to carry on being be a Town Hall wallah. He was reserved[6] and too important to die.

But there was a War on, so once a week he had to go with his wooden rifle to do Home Guard duty at Ladybower, to stop the parachuting Germans weeing in our drinking water.

He also went off in a lorry with *The Guild Variety Players* to do a magic trick with his stooge, for the troops out in Derbyshire, before they went off to die.

What he did for that was fold a piece of paper, chew it, swallow it, pass it down his tummy and his leg, under the stage, and up his stooge's leg and tummy then into the stooge's mouth so when the stooge stuck out his tongue there was the folded piece of paper on it. The paper then travelled back down the stooge, under the floor and up my Dad till it was on his tongue.

The troops always said Dad had to do it again, so he always did. But this time the stooge always messed it up, so that both he and Dad ended up with chewed-up spitty bits of paper on their tongues when they stuck them out.

Then Dad sang his song:

> *I met a girl out West one night*
> *She had a very fine appetite!*

His song was called *4 and 9* and what happened in it was, Dad took this girl out for her tea to Lockhart's in the Strand, and -

> *I counted my money and I'd 4 and 9,*
> *4 and 9,*
> *4 and 9!*

She ate and drank so much that he couldn't pay, so she went home and left him to do the washing up.

The moral of the song is don't invite girls out to tea because they are only after your *4 and 9*.[7]

---

6 He was too young to fight the Great War till the last few weeks. He joined the Navy, and got as far as Crystal Palace. The only time he was in peril was when a sailor in the bunk below tried to tickle him. He never forgot that, and warned us it could happen to us.
7 23p.

He also sang *Excelsior* in two parts, and that was about -

> *A youth who bore, mid snow and ice,*
> *A banner with the strange device,*
> *Excelsior!*

Nobody knew what it meant, but it was sad.

The Guild Variety Players were all Town Hall wallahs. One of their programmes went -

---

The Guild Variety Players Present

'Camp Variety'

As played to HM Forces (VES)
And produced by Austyn Mettam

Opening Chorus –	The Girls
Madge or Cliff –	In Song
Reg Greenwood –	Magical moments
China Town –	The Austyn Girls
Ann Taylor –	Our Contralto
Our Film Studio –	Muriel, Gethin, Reg, George
Madge and Cliff –	Duets
The Gavotte –	The Girls
Violin and Piano –	Addy and Bill
Muriel Gay –	In Tap and Tempo
Geo Shaw –	?????
Madge and Cliff –	More duets
Our Military Number –	The Austyn Girls
Music Hall	

The King

Management –	S. Gethin Robinson
Compere –	Reg Greenwood

At Christmas, instead of *Camp Variety,* the troops got Santa Claus and we were allowed to watch. Every time, five minutes after Santa waved bye bye, and went out to his reindeer, Dad came back in from making a phone call to The Office, and took us home to Totley.

Can You Create My Memoirs?

You can!

Read this book in any order!

If it's getting boring, go somewhere else! [8]

---

8 Or just read the footnotes. They're more indiscreet.

Chandler, Lily

My Mum only had one name.

Her brothers and sisters had loads of names, especially her younger sister who had so many she never knew what to call herself.[9]

My Mum was *Lily* after an Aunty Lily in Sidmouth or *Lillian* sometimes in programmes, because people who give a lifetime's service to the amateur theatre movement have to have funny names e.g. Lillian Meeke, Austyn Mettam and S. Gethin Robinson.

Anyway, Lily never liked being Lily.[10] It was before Lily Allen, so in those days being *Lily* was like being *Ivy* or *Primrose*, and it rhymed with *silly* and - I don't really know why she didn't like her name, but she didn't, and some people don't.

What she did like was the slightly older man she met at Timpson's corner,[11] and the play he took her to when she was 23.

She also liked Keep Fit, and playing netball for Yorkshire and cricket for Sheffield. I think she used to like the *Women's League of Health and Beauty* as well.

She also liked keeping a diary, walking, swimming, cricket, crosswords, gardening, and knitting pullovers.

Most of all she liked teaching. She'd been to college in London to learn how to do it. But then after eight years she suddenly got married to the man from Timpson's corner, and stopped teaching for ever, because married women weren't allowed.

She didn't agree with that because she was a bit of a feminist. And that was also why she didn't like washing, ironing, drying, dusting, hoovering, and polishing, though she did it all.[12]

---

9 When she died aged 100 nobody was sure who she had been.
10 Yet her children, and grandchildren all called her Lily. And still do when we talk about her, which we do a lot.
11 I interviewed her about her life just after Dad died. Neither of us heard what we were saying. I've never listened to the tape. But I'm pretty sure they first met when he went to pay the wages at the school she was teaching at, and he asked her to meet him at Timpson's corner, so that he could take her to see him in a play at the Little Theatre in Shipton Street. I'm not sure she was 23.
12 My daughter Megan adds, 'She told me it was like threading beads on a piece of string with no knot at the end.'

I helped when I got a bit bigger because I was a bit of a feminist too. Dad wasn't, because he was a bit scared of women and all that.[13] Though he was never scared of Lily.

When he died after more than fifty years together she wrote in her diary -

> *This is the unhappiest day of my life.*

*

But my Mum and Dad had their differences.

She wrote all the diaries, and all the family letters in careful curly handwriting. Dad, the municipal officer clerk, was illegible, like all his sons would turn out to be.

She read novels. He took the *Daily Herald* and made it last all day.

She didn't sing. He did.

She didn't believe in God. He was a cathedral choirboy and a Mason.

She didn't drive. He did.

She was a socialist. He wasn't.

She was United. He was Wednesday.

She liked to ramble in the countryside. He liked to amble in the suburbs looking into windows, and wondering who was living in the houses he should have bought, instead of still renting from Mr Laver.

They didn't agree about much, and never disagreed about anything. They never raised their voices.[14]

But they did have two big secrets.

*

---

13 And so would you have been, if a sailor had tried to tickle you at Crystal Palace. And if you'd met a girl who was only after your 4 and 9. And if you had an older sister like Auntie Gwenny, who was always cross. And if what happened with Edna had happened to you, of course - but more of her later.

14 One of my marriage guidance counsellors suggested it would have been better if they had, so I'd not be so scared of having rows with my partners.

After the Germans had bombed the *Marples*,[15] and after Dad recovered from his pneumonia, and after the War started properly, Mum was allowed to be a teacher again.

So Mrs Allison had to look after me at 11 Aldam Road on the Council Estate. Her house smelt of gas. She had a monkey-puzzle tree to scare kids on winter afternoons, when they were about to walk home alone in the dark and get kidnapped and shaved and given a number by the orphanage up Mickley Lane.

Mum did most of her teaching at Sharrow Lane, which was a school for poor children who weren't supposed to go to grammar schools. But she helped them to go anyway because she was a socialist. She was an Old Girl of Abbeydale Girls Grammar School[16] as well, so it was easy for her to teach even the hardest hard things like -

> *Their hats, their cats,*
> *Their balls, their bats,*
> *T. H. E. I. R.*
> *There is, there are,*
> *There was, there were,*
> *T. H. E. R. E.*

She knew all the hardest tables -

> *Seven eights are fifty-six*
> *Eights sevens are fifty-six too*
> *Nine sevens are sixty three*

She understood commas in the air denoting possession or omission, and the one exception -

> *The cat licked it (no apostrophe) s tail.*
> *But it (apostrophe) s a nice day*
> *(But we don (apostrophe) t say nice.)*

---

15 December 12 1940. The night Dad didn't dive. A bright moonlight night. The sirens went off at 7 pm. Scores of people hid in the cellars of the Marples pub in Fitzalan Square. At 11.44 pm a bomb plunged through the seven storeys and exploded. The Marples was never actually called The Marples. The Germans code named their Blitz on Sheffield – 'Crucible'. 64 bodies were identified. Dad would have been one, but for his tickle.

16 Supported after she was 15 by bursaries of £8 and £10 that she won from the Education Committee.

Her three star pupils were called Jimmy Green, who went to King Edward's, but we don't know if anything happened to him after, and Janet Howarth, who went to the High School, and we met her in Scarborough at the open-air theatre, after she'd gone posh.

Lily's third star pupil was Stephen McClarence who went to High Storrs and York University and came home to write for *The Star*. When he met her in the Crucible Studio years later he never went out for his journalist's free red wine, but stayed talking with her all interval.

Most people who ring me about Lily tell me she was strict but fair. Though, to be strictly fair, some say she was fair but strict. I say she broke a plate over my head when I was seven and slapped my arm when I was nine, but fair enough, if that was all she ever did wrong to me, ever.[17]

She was the only mother on the Laverdene who ever went out to work. She never wore make-up or stockings, but she used opadeldoch[18] on her hands when they went squawky with school chalk. She had a bath every Sunday afternoon, and when she came downstairs, she said she felt

> *Like Burke's best!*[19]

*

The other thing about my Mum is that she was murdered.

I was still at junior school.

I saw it.

She was in a wheelchair, even if she didn't need one.

And this man called Danny had come to live with her because he had made her maid have a baby last August Bank Holiday. Everything was going all right till a human hand was found in the dustbin and then a woman's cut-off head was found in a hatbox, and I think it was the maid's.[20]

Danny was Welsh so everybody liked him, and this other girl loved him. I think my Mum loved him too. But when it started to get dark, we guessed he was the murderer, because he talked to himself in the mirror. He was guilty

---

17 It was, except my name, and she of all people should have known better about names.
18 You spell it then.
19 I think Burke's was a tailor. Or a brewery.
20 Head, not hatbox.

but insane, and that was why he cut off people's hands and heads, and smothered my Mum with a cushion off the settee and only took nine seconds.

There's no need to be frightened though, because it was only a play called *Night Must Fall* that the TOADS[21] often did.

My Mum was always in TOADS plays. There were always TOADS words to be underlined, learned and tested. There was always a TOADS rehearsal on Tuesday nights, and the twice-a-year panic that this was going to be the worst TOADS show ever, though it always turned out to be the best.

She mainly did character parts, which means you aren't important enough in a play for anything to happen to you to change you, so you can just act daft. She was nuns, landladies who warmed their bottoms on the pretend fire, ghosts, and maids.

As a TOAD she got drunk, talked posh, and once went mad in Frecheville.

She kissed men who weren't my Dad, and said she loved them. We knew she didn't mean it,[22] but the audience didn't, because she was so good at acting.

In very old age she prompted from a shaky stool, perched nearly out of sight behind the flats, like Burke's best, strict but fair, and louder than any of them, so that the audience could always tell whose fault it was when nobody was speaking or someone had started speaking the same things all over again.

She never acted in any of my plays, and I wish she had.[23]

*

The twice-a-year TOADS are still at it of course.

People still stride onto Totley stages to introduce themselves to people who already know them. They still suddenly sit and stand and face the wrong way, and still can't perform normal tasks like pouring sherry, or opening doors. They still live in country houses and still can't move for all the unmatching furniture, as if the Duke of Devonshire has been transplanted to Darnall in some secret socialist revolution and no one's noticed that even his curtains won't shut any more. Or that his vast unearned estates have gone

---

21 The Totley Operatic and Dramatic Society.

22 Geth teased her and called her Lily the Actor, in the big advert he wrote (and paid for) in The Star for her ninetieth birthday. He never missed a show, though, if she could help it.

23 And I've also never really written about her till now either.

two-dimensional and have to be squeezed past, because his French windows will never open again.

The strangest people still get it together at the TOADS, breaking deep Totley taboos of age, class and gender, on stage and off.

And they're always looking for new members, because they still keep getting murdered.

Charity

All the author's royalties (x 2) from this book go to the Children's Hospital, which was Radio Sheffield's charity last year.

I shyly[24] suggested doing my memoirs to the BBC last year instead of karaoke or ballroom dancing. Everyone responded brilliantly.

Alistair immediately said he'd publish it, and match my royalties (hence, x 2). John Palmer was immediately up for a big launch at Hallam.

Off The Shelf backed it after one text message.

Radio Sheffield immediately suggested the radio programmes that go with it.

And The Children's Hospital were straight in of course.

Steve McClarence and Francis Byrnes read an early draft and were wise and kind.

Goronwy Thom did the unpaid photo shoot for the cover, this summer, and that was a new father/son bonding thing for us.

The whole project has turned out to be more fun (to do) than karaoke and ballroom dancing.

It's taken me to strange places.

And because I get absolutely nothing from it, even the paper and ink, I've not felt quite so bad thinking and writing about myself for most of this year.

£2 from every book goes straight to charity, remember? Be charitable! Buy one for a friend!

24 Slyly?

Daddy Robinson

Mr Ronksley wrote from Beechwood Road Hillsborough, February 1997 -

> *Dear Sir,*
>
> *One of my friends recently told me you had been speaking on the radio about your grandfather, Wadsley Church of England School Headmaster Mr Samuel Whitehouse Robinson.*
>
> *I was a scholar there from 1922 until 1931.*
>
> *In the early 1920s I believe he lived in a stone-built house just above the Old Admiral Rodney public house. During that time he used to walk over Rodney Hill along Rural Lane. On bad weather days using his umbrella mainly as a walking stick. On fine days just the walking stick.*
>
> *When Mr Robinson assembled us for singing, his two favourites were Men of Harlech and Who is Sylvia? And two posh words we all learned were diminuendo and crescendo.*
>
> *In my later years I used to wonder if he was a Welshman. I still don't know.*[25]
>
> *We played football on the Wadsley Common using Wadsley Church's pitch. If he came to watch us play he would encourage us or criticise us using our surnames.*
>
> *If your father or uncles were there they dared not say anything.*

Mr Ronksley added that Samuel Whitehouse moved to Vainor Road, and retired in late 1930.

Another listener told me the kids called him *Daddy Robinson.*[26]

I don't know much more about him except that he came from Dudley, trained at Cheltenham, and was Headmaster at Wadsley C of E for almost all his working life.

---

25 He wasn't.
26 His own kids called him 'Pa' and their Mum 'Ma'.

Oh, and that somehow he wasn't properly pensioned. When he suddenly died in hospital trying to get a fellow-patient back into bed, Nanny Robbo was left so poor she had to defraud the trams and wear black, and drink Guinness to keep up her blood.

On the school photos listeners sent, Samuel Whitehouse looks like my Dad, and Our Geth, and now me, though stouter and smaller. He is a sporty snappy dresser, very proud of his waxy moustache. My Dad and Our Geth were sporty and snappy too, though neither ever managed any facial hair.[27]

---

27 Except on one week in Anglesey when I persuaded Dad to grow a moustache, and it was bristly and grey, and so frightened Nanny Robbo when we went round to Milden Road on the Sunday after, taking her a souvenir pencil from Llanffairbgogggygoggy, she had to have a Guinness for her blood, there and then.

Dolly, Lily, Pussy, Leon, Mary, Billy, Denis, Gwenny, Gethin, Trevor, Blodwen, Goronwy and Olwen.

Nanny Chandler lived with Grandy Chandler in a small smallholding at Woodhouse with a small duck pond to fall in.

Then she lived in a bungalow up Long Line in Dore, but it snowed.

Then she moved to a bungalow in Crosspool to be near Uncle Leon and the blind people.

Then she went to Beighton to be near the chip shop and Aunty Dolly.

Then she died, but Grandy Chandler had already died.

There were loads of other Chandlers including Dolly, Lily, my Mum, Pussy, Leon and Mary. And two other brothers nobody talked about.

All our cousins were on Nanny Chandler's side.

They were Roy, Clive and Barbara who lived at Woodhouse with Aunty Dolly and she smoked Park Drives in the kitchen and had a harmonium that smelt of Jesus' empty tomb when you pedalled it.

Glyn and Garry were our cousins who lived with Aunty Pussy in Birmingham. She found their dad at a bus stop on Snig Hill.

Uncle Leon in Crosspool had Little Leon, then Billy, then Sarah, with his wife Aunty Bessie, who laughed at him even when he wasn't being funny.

Paul Mann[28] and his three brothers lived with Aunty Mary at Gleadless, then at Robin Hoods Bay. They were mad on bikes and called themselves *The Family of Mann.*

We all went to Nanny Chandler's for turkey on Christmas Day. But Aunty Dolly's children were only allowed for tea. Barbara baked a bright green cake and everyone said it was nice.

---

28 The man(n) who does more to hold the Chandlers together than most.

At Christmas, Grandy Chandler played *My Grandfather's Clock* and *The Volunteer Organist* on his piano in the front room while the women washed up.

The Volunteer Organist was about this old tramp who had to play the organ in church one day because the real organist was ill. Everyone thought he shouldn't, but when he did it was wonderful.

> *The scene was one I'll ne'er forget*
> *As long as I may live*
> *And just to see it one more time*
> *All earthly joys I'd give.*

My Grandfather's Clock was about a grandfather who died because his grandfather clock stopped. Grandy's nose ran when he sang as loud as he dared, hoping Nanny Chandler would be sorry when he stopped and died.[29]

*

Nanny Robbo lived near Sheffield Wednesday at Milden Road, at the end of the Middlewood tram, up a dark hill, and through three black jennels with big trees with slippy roots.

My Dad could have played for Sheffield Wednesday, but he was a singer too, so he went to be Head Choirboy at Ripon[30] instead. He was a pupil at Jepson's School there and in the 1911 census he was 10 years old, and their youngest boarder. By 1912 he was in Form IV getting second prize for General Subjects and Singing.[31]

Aunty Gwenny always lived with Nanny Robbo and was always cross. Nanny Robbo was always Welsh[32] and always put her hands up boys' trousers.

Anyway, Nanny Robbo and Aunty Gwenny had to share the double bed at the front after Pa died, because they had to have lodgers. The lodgers were kept

---

29 And, strangely, she was

30 I had my first curry in Ripon, at 15, when Dad took us to a Choir reunion. An old boy recognised him there 50 years on, because his feet were like a sailor's even before Crystal Palace. Three years ago I sat in his Head Choirboy's chair in the Minster, and sang O For The Wings Of A Dove very quietly, and pretended I was him.

31 At 6 Laverdene, my Dad always sang his own words, about himself, to old hymn tunes and bits of Gilbert and Sullivan. My daughter Megan asks, 'Have you written anything about him singing around the house? About how beautiful and sweet he was? And how you do it now and how we love it and sometimes hate it?'

32 Which is why there are still so many Welsh names in our family and why we are so full of hwyl.

in the downstairs back room with the green furry tassly tablecloth and also in the bedroom next to the lavatory that had a rostrum, and smelt of Vim and old wee.

On Thursday nights, Nanny Robbo used to put on her black hat with a pin, and catch the Middlewood tram to the Town Hall, but she only ever paid to Snig Hill, and then stared at the conductor. She then went to *Hays Wine Lodge,* and kept her hat on to drink Guinnesses with a woman called *Mrs Noneofyourbusinesses.*

Then she got the tram and stared all the way back to Middlewood, and never paid at all.

*

We Robinsons started to die out after 1945.

Aunty Gwenny couldn't get married because of her phenobarbitone and her wig, and the blood oath she had made with her girlfriends at teachers' college. But they all did get married of course, and she was cross about that. When Nanny Robbo died, Aunty Gwenny broke her own blood oath, and paid an agency to find her a man with a car, and got married after all. But she still couldn't have any children because she was 66, and I expect she was cross about that too.

My Uncle Goronwy never married, had no children and died, even if his photo stayed on Nanny Robbo's piano going brown till 1974.

Uncle Trevor lived in Matlock Bath in a cottage that only had three walls. There wasn't room for children and anyway he had his hernia they couldn't cure even when he went to the USSR. I think that Uncle Trevor's hernia was why Aunty Olive Ran Off. My Dad said he shouldn't have let her Run Back after. But he did, and I don't blame him because when Aunty Olive kissed you, you didn't mind like you do with your other aunties, and she chuckled, and tickled.

When she died, Uncle Trevor kept all her clothes and prostheses and medicines in a cupboard and slept on her side of their double bed in Lytham St Annes.

Aunty Blodwen died when she was a baby so she had no babies. Aunty Olwen was a hairdresser who lived with Uncle Charlie three doors up from Nanny Robbo on Milden Road. He was Scotch and they smoked Capstan cigarettes, and had Scotch and peppermint in bottles. They forgot to feed their cat, or pick their apples in their garden, so I suppose they just forgot to make their babies too.

And that's why the Robinsons were starting to die out after 1945, once Our Dave was born.

Dave - The Souvenir

It was Whitsuntide 1944, and Nanny Chandler declared that the War in Europe was over, and took a taxi to Thornwick Bay to re-open her caravan. It was made out of an old tram and smelt of boys' bottoms.

We followed her on a Sheffield United coach to Bridlington.

When I saw the sea I asked where the bridge was.

There was barbed wire all along the cliffs, and I thought it was the skeleton of blackberry bushes from last year.

We waded out in our droopy costumes into the fishy caves at North Landing, and weed purple through them onto the seaweed.

We drank Oxo in the Café on the way to Bempton, which said Café on its roof for the seagulls, even if it shouldn't have, in case the Germans came back.

It didn't rain all the time, and it didn't matter if it did.

Our Dave was a souvenir from Thornwick Bay, and the following February he was born in our front bedroom.[33]

I knew he was coming because Nanny Jessop had trudged over from Lemont Road again and asked me if I'd decided to be a boy or a girl yet. Then Dr Marshall arrived for his whisky, and got cross about the National Health Service that was going to make Sheffield like Russia. There was a lot of water running in the lav all night, and in the morning Our Dave was there, only he was called Michael then.

Because of him I had to give up the box room and share the back bedroom with our Geth for ever, and that wasn't fair because he'd already got the window you could see the Orphanage from, and it was me who got told off when he was wheezy.

And I had to go to school as well.

---

[33] Like me. My Mum and Dad both died at 6 Laverdene too. So, one conception, two births and two deaths in 64 years.

Dads Cry

Dad took me on the first day[34] and left me crying there, at

All Saints Church of England Mixed Infant, Junior and Senior School,
Hillfoot Road,
Totley,
Derbyshire,
Sheffield,
Yorkshire,
England,
Great Britain,
The United Kingdom,
Europe,
Northern Hemisphere,
The Earth,
The Globe,
The Planets,
The Solar System,
The Universe,
Eternity.

It was pigshit.

---

34 I took my own son Goronwy to the same school on his first day, and cried again.

Do Try These At Home
Nine things you can do after reading this book, all royalties from which go to charity (x2)

Imagine your own conception!

Have three sassy children without really trying!

Get in *The News of the World!*

Meet dozens of famous people!

Meet a *Sex and Royalty Editor!*

Donate sperm!

Die!

Meet a man who cremated himself!

Stand in front of fifteen thousand fellow citizens, and two bishops, as planes drop from the sky and the clock goes backwards![35]

---

35 My daughter Megan says to add, 'With your two children giggling at your side at the Millennium - me and Gron right there with you.'

Down The Road From Nanny Robbo

Roy Hattersley, the MP - the one who had the dog called Buster, and once appeared on television as a tub of lard - used to live just down the road from Nanny Robbo.

His Mum used to be called *Enid Hattersley,* and she was noisy.[36]

Someone else who was noisy was an opera signer named *Peter Glossop*[37] after Glossop Road baths. He sang at the bottom of Nanny Robbo's garden and you could hear him over the Wednesday fans at Owlerton every other Saturday.

I never heard any Hattersleys sing.

---

36 I've never interviewed Roy Hattersley, but I did have dinner with him at a Derbyshire literary festival, just after he had gone vegetarian. I should have interviewed him some years before at a Doncaster literary festival but he didn't turn up. I interviewed Enid on the radio, though, when she was very old but still very noisy. She kept telling everyone off for smoking even when we weren't. In 1968 Roy Hattersley's wife Mrs Hattersley interviewed me for a job at Kidbroke Girls' School. She had big glasses. I got the impression men didn't impress her much. I didn't get the job. Roy Hattersley's old headmaster R. H. Davies had gone from City Grammar in Sheffield to Eltham Green SE9 and he interviewed me, for my first job in teaching. He talked to me about Roy Hattersley whenever he recognised me in the staff room for the next seven years. There was another Roy Hattersley altogether who had nothing to do with Nanny Robbo's Roy Hattersley, though he was also a Labour Councillor in Sheffield. I never interviewed him, either.
37 I interviewed him decades later and he remembered Nanny Robbo.

DJ Rony – the Truth

Our Geth, my older brother, was really called *Gethin* after my Dad who was called *Samuel Gethin* after his Mum, whose surname used to be Gethin when she was in Wales.

Our Geth was also called *Leon* after my Mum's Dad who was called *Leon* after a famous president no one's heard of called *Leon Gambetta*.

My Dad and Mum's families had loads of these great names like *Gethin* and *Leon Gambetta, Gwendolyn, Lois, Leonora, Lincoln, Olwen* and *Blodwen*.

But I was called *John* and Our Dave was called *Michael*.

John and *Michael* were common.

Mum changed Our Dave from *Michael* to *David* when the other kids started calling him *Mick,* but I stayed *John* until Grammar school, when I stopped having a name and was just *Robinson*.

Luckily, though, my full name included *Goronwy* because of my Uncle *Goronwy.* He was known in the Robinson family as *Rony*.

So when we started having names again, I decided I'd be *Rony*.

I still have to be *John* when I'm in hospital, of course, or at the hygienist's, or dead. But that's good because then I can pretend I'm not me, when they tell me to floss more, or that it's my own fault for drinking so much.

Ronys aren't common.

Google us! Facebook us!

We are beautiful Israeli brunettes, American models, a woman singer in Ohio, a retired basketball hero, a Lebanese percussionist, a juggler, a Malaysian boy, a Christian Revivalist in Manila, and a French cyclist.

And a DJ in Dhaka.

The only other *Rony Robinson* on *Facebook* in the entire beautiful world is a beautiful young military man in Chile, who wouldn't add me as his friend when I asked.

2. There I Met A Monkey

Down Hillfoot Road

Saints aren't all saints, e.g.

Matthew Mark Luke and John
Went to bed with their trousers on

We had Miss Marsden in the Infants at our All Saints. She was very old and you didn't want her to touch you, in case she was dead.

Then we had Mrs Horsefield who was a widow like Widow Twankey at the Lyceum so you didn't want her to touch you either.

Then we had Miss Freeborough. We dropped our pencils and looked up her legs, and she smacked the tops of ours, but then she changed into Mrs Glatt and left.

There was a Miss Jones we didn't have, who cried. And there was a Miss Goldsbrough who was olive and black. Our Dave still loves her.[38]

We had Old Barrett who rulered us on the knuckles in the Chapel and told us there wasn't a Father Christmas.[39] He also explained the Trinity (but no one got it) and how to spell parallelogram (but no one could) and how it's treble not threble, and that you are never allowed to start sentences with And or But or So.

But not long after, someone saw him serving drinks outside the South Seas in Broomhill.

So something must have happened.

And after Old Barrett, we had Old Ma Peacock. It was her job to make us Pass the Scholarship, so she had to teach us e.g. for example, and how you can get confused because, e.g., for example, isn't the same as i.e. She took the punctuation out of things as well, and then made us put it back, e.g.

havent you read charles kingsleys westward ho the teacher mrs
peacock said[40]

---

38 He is a Cliff Richard fan too, and a Blade, even if he lives in Essex and is very rich, which is a bit rich since he only Passed to High Storrs, and didn't shine there, except with girls on the Roughs, and with one he took bilberrying on Totley Moss.
39 There is a Father Christmas. I think the Trinity is more unlikely, myself.
40 Don't try it at home but I think it is - "Haven't you read Charles Kingsley's 'Westward Ho!'?" the teacher, Mrs Peacock, said.

If you Failed the Scholarship you had to stay on in the Seniors and have Bert Shirt and learn lettuces and swimming, or Old Hodgkiss, who was called Herbert, because of his song the Seniors sang in the playground, i.e.

> *Ta ra ra boom di ay*
> *Old Herbert trumped today!*
> *He blew his books away*
> *Ta ra ra boom di ay!*

We had other songs in our playground too, e.g.

> *In and out the dusky bluebells*
> *You shall be my partner!*

And -

> *The good ship sails through the alley alley oh*
> *The alley alley oh*
> *The alley alley oh!*

There was a rude one that ended -

> *Uncle Jim makes lemonade*
> *Round the corner chocolate's made!*

When the teacher was shouting at playtime somewhere else in the playground with their cup of tea with the saucer on top, we used rude words like, e.g.

> *Bloody!*
> *And bum!*
> *And bloody bum!*
> *And pigshit!*
> *And bloody bum and bloody pigshit!*

*

Our Headmaster was called Mr S. Mellor, i.e. Old Smellor.

He came out of town every day, and spoke in Yorkshire. The other teachers imitated him when he wasn't listening and he never listened anyway. He was the only person allowed to interrupt the prayers, e.g.

Our Feather
Keep up Dixon Harper!
Witch heart in Devon
I shan't tell thee again Pat Taylor!
Harold be thy gnome
Keep up Fred Webster!
Viking drum drum
Thank you Alan Otter!
Fly wheel be dumb
I said I shan't tell thee again Pat Taylor!
In Perth as it is in Devon

Old Smellor wore threble-breasted royal blue suits, with fat chalk stripes, and his teeth slipped at assembly, e.g.

Awake my soul and with the shglshun!

He parked his square powder-blue Standard Vanguard Ten[41] with the globe stuck in its square bonnet in our playground, and caned us when we gozzed on it. And he told lies too, e.g.

Not in my shgool you don't!

But it wasn't his school.

It was Stanley Moffatt, Director of Education's's school because it said so on the front of our grey exercise books with the tables on the back saying, e.g.

10 chains one furlong
8 furlongs one mile
2 gills one peck

All Saints School also belonged to All Saints Church, down Cow Flop Lane. The Vicar there was called Old Adamson, which was a good name for a Vicar. His daughter went to a paying school, so he never visited ours.

*

41 Our Dave read these memoirs and corrected this to a Triumph Mayflower.

We had May Days, which meant we had our own Queen, and she was
Maureen Hughes from the Seniors.[42] And we had a Maypole when we did
A Hundred Pipers and were allowed to touch girls' waists.

Some of the people in my class were called Nigel Graham Gregory and
Hewson Charles Thomas Fawcett and Frank Michael Humpherson Jones.
And Gillian Hall and Gillian Gall.[43]

Philip Rodney Andrew once said to me -

> *If you say, God's Honour you'll never tell no one never, you can*
> *come with us after school to those trees off of Baslow Road and look*
> *at me and my girl friend Janet, if you want?*

I did, so I did, and I did, and I haven't.

My girl friend was Janet too, only she wasn't the same Janet.[44]

> *She loves me she don't!*
> *She will, she won't!*

We bounced together up the steps from the playground -

> *I went up one stair*
> *Just like me!*
> *I went up two stairs*
> *Just like me!*

But right at the top you had to go -

> *There I met a monkey*
> *Just like me!*

The girls got me in Kisscatch and Choosing, e.g.

> *King William was King David's son*
> *All the royal races run*
> *Choose from the east and choose from the west*
> *Choose the one that you love best.*

---

42 I never dared speak but years later I am in The Cricket, and she's serving on. She calls,
'Hello John!' I'm not John, but I don't mind her saying I am, because it means she remembers
me from when I was.
43 Two gills one peck. True, spread it.
44 She was Janet Smith, the dinner lady's daughter. She had to go to the clinic for her heart
every Friday. It must have worked, because fifty years later when we spoke on the radio, she
was alive in Low Edges.

At All Saints, when you got a card with a green corner in the register it meant Extraction on Leopold Street, with no breakfast because they were going to gas you with a rubber mask.

In Marsdens after, you could get blood in your milk shake if you blew down the straw instead of sucking.

We had to put cotton wool in our ears in the winter to stop the wax leaking. Some kids wobbled, and some had lazy eyes, and one girl rocked. Two boys had things on their ankles because they had polio, and some kids broke their arms and had to have plasters, but they weren't allowed to write on them.

The kids from the orphanage up Mickley got impetigo and nits and had to be painted, but we didn't.

Podge Turton had webbed fingers, and some people had their tonsils out and one kid got circumnavigated by Dr. Marshall. Some kids had funny lips, and broken noses and different ears and gumboils and verrucas and styes, and they were usually from the orphanage as well.

But nobody ever died.

*

School dinners came at quarter past nine in the morning in a square grey van called School Meals that smelt of plimsolls and TCP.

There was never enough dinner except when it was stew with turnip.

Once we had gravy with lettuce and caterpillars.

*

In J2 I learned to skip and play conkers.

And to wee over the dubs into the playground.[45]

I also learned PLP?

> *Are you a PLP?*
> *No!*
> *Then you're not a proper looking person!*
> *Ow!*

---

45 Nearly. Once.

Or -

> *Are you a PLP?*
> *Yes then!*
> *Then you're a public leaning post!*
> *Ow!*

I know how to get out of PLP. (Only I've forgotten.)

I had three fights, one with Patrick Wortley by mistake.

But I know how to get out of fights.

You go -

> *Wanna feight?*

And they go -

> *Yes!*

So you go -

> *I'll hold your coat!*

Sometimes then they hit you and go -

> *Heard it!*
> *Ow!*

Or -

> *Tell us news not ancient history!*
> *Ow!*

So then you go -

> *Wanna feight?*
> *Yes!*
> *Seven! Gerrit?*[46]

---

46 1 off 8 = 7. Get it?

Once I went into the air-raid shelter where the Senior boys smoked Wild Woodbines and watched the Senior girls lift up their dresses instead of having Dinner, but you couldn't see anything because of the smoke.

*

Our worst hymn in assembly was -

> *There is a green hill far away without a city wall*

- because you could see Old Smellor's's breakfast when he sang it, and also because the hymn was mental because everyone knows hills don't have walls.[47]

Once upon a time, though, Miss Freeborough took us on a Nature Walk to the curly river in the big field, and that does have a wall, between the *Crown* and the Akky.

We dangled in the curly river and she read us *Tom Sawyer.*

That was the happiest I ever was at any school ever.

> *'Now, Becky, it's all done - all over but the kiss. Don't you be afraid of that - it ain't anything at all. Please, Becky.' And he tugged at her apron.*

> *By and by she gave up, and let her hands drop. Her face, all glowing with the struggle, came up and submitted.*

> *Tom kissed the red lips and said, 'Now it's all done, Becky. And always after this, you know, you ain't ever to love anybody but me, and you ain't ever to marry anybody but me, ever never and forever. Will you?'*

*

I broke a window in J2 by chucking a snowball with a piece of coke in it. I never told when I saw Brian Horsefield getting got for it. Even his mother, even if she was a widow and a teacher, could not save him from Old Smellor's slashing cane right across your writing fingers, so you wet yourself and cry at the same time, which is dangerous, and makes you hate teachers for ever.

---

47 And Greenhill isn't far away either because our Seniors always lost to them at football 23-nil and 38-4 except at home when it was 1-46.

I was caned by Old Smellor for buying windfall apples from the cottage next to the school at four-a-penny because he'd told us not to, only he hadn't.

> *Bum to old Smellor!*
> *Gozz on his car!*

We played mabs when it was the mab season and one day in J3 we were up on the Pinfold going -

> *Jinx!*
> *Na fibs na fabs!*
> *Tha's lost thi mabs!*

And I saw Patsy Otter trap Our Dave in the corner where the boys' dubs met the Pinfold, and he called -

> *Let me go Patsy!*

But she didn't.[48]

*

For J3 and J4 I was in Old Ma Peacocks's in the Horsy Hut. She was from Totley Rise Methodists so she shouldn't have been in our Church of England school anyway. But she was the only teacher who never hit us.[49]

She practised the Eleven Plus all the time, except on Wednesday afternoon when we had to sing -

> *Now the day is over*
> *Night is drawing nigh*

She made me sit right at the back of the Horsy Hut for all of J4, looking out over Totley Bents, watching the last year of weather.

> *Shadows of the evening*
> *Creep across the sky.*

I was top of her class in her Intelligence Tests but I turned over two pages in the Eleven Plus exam. Old Smellor said in front of all the assembly that -

---

48 My daughter Megan adds, 'Tell how you still tell this story in Anglesey every year.'
49 I said that on Radio Sheffield and Christopher Needham's's sister wrote in to say, 'Oh yes she did!'

That weren't very intelligent John Goronwy were it?

And he also said -

John Goronwy didn't gerr' on wi' it did he, schglool?[50]

But he Appealed.

And I Passed.

So I had to go to King Edward's anyway.

*

On the last afternoon of our childhoods, Mrs Peacock let me do a play I had written called *Dead Men Live Again* in front of all the class. It was about a criminal whose escape was announced on the radio but who then turned up in our shed. She said I was obviously going to be a playwright when I grew up.

And that was goodbye Little John Robinson, girls, and Totley.

---

50 Gerrit?

Down Our Way

Totley isn't the same as Dore, even if some people think it is, just because when they arrive at our station it says -

Dore and Totley [51]

But they're not the same e.g. Totley Brook Road isn't in Totley, it's in Dore.

And the brook that runs along Totley Brook Road isn't Totley Brook, it's Old Hay Brook. Totley Brook is the brook that is in Totley, and curls through Gilly Woods full of bullyheads, sticklebacks, bendy trout and soapstones.

The bridge over Old Hay Brook on Baslow Road (which isn't in Baslow) has writing showing that that is where Totley and Dore parishes have always met in the middle of the river. But Totley only got its own church in 1928 so it's not always been always at all.

*

My Dad's headed notepaper for his Hillsborough Lodge Freemasons said -

> *Laverdene Drive*
> *Dore*
> *Sheffield*

It must have been a mistake at the printers, because Laverdene, where there once were monkey gardens and rhubarb fields, is on the other side of Baslow Road from Dore, and so much in Totley it's nearly in Bradway.

*

Dore has a men's club, a male voice choir, a gala, well dressings and a toy soldier on its village green. And a sheep roast and a proper garage with petrol pumps, and lord mayors, and footballers and entrepreneurs who go to jail. And a battle.

But Totley has a proper library, not just a bus, and more churches, schools, people, and pubs. Totley Drinkers still do the Totley Ten, which means having a pint in all ten Totley pubs, even in those that aren't there any more.

---

51 Dore and Totley Station as is, and was, but for years was only Dore (to save money for Dr. Beeching) isn't in Dore or Totley. It's in Abbeydale, like the Abbeydale Garden Centre (as was) isn't but was.

And who wants a battle anyway?[52]

The Top of Totley is still sometimes called The Village because it still has its pinfold, stone schools, school house, stone halls and lodges, stone cottages, bobby's row and, in once-upon-times, a post office, bus terminus with its own clock on a stick, stocks, and sudden countryside from when Totley was in Derbyshire, and the Summer Lane folk talked in tups, tegs and wethers.

Totley Tunnel, 3.5 miles, is the longest non-electric train tunnel in England. It is the most famous thing ever to come out of Totley. But it doesn't come out in Totley at either end of itself.

No one knows where Totley stops, even Brian Edwards and the Totley History Group, and they know everything, because added up they are older than Totley. Once you get a bike (mine was a black Hercules with sit-up-and beg handlebars, no gears, a bell, and a little saddlebag, with its own John Bull repair kit[53] with chalk, and valves and an aluminium spanner) Totley stretches to Twentywell, the Brickworks, the Orphanage, and Tinker's Corner.

---

52 And it wasn't a battle anyway.
53 A friend who read an early version of this said that I'd got it wrong - John Bull did printing sets. Indeed they did. Fred Pass in Weerz Me Dad (p14 ff) tells the most wonderful tale of his gang using a set to stamp rude messages on a baby and some bananas. But there were John Bull repair kits as well, in long light blue tins, and I had one, with valves.

Evensongs Down Cowflop Lane

I joined All Saints Church when I was eight years old because I wanted the black dress with the eleven woolly buttons that the choir had to wear on Hash Wednesdays.

Hash Wednesdays were when our school had to march in a crocodile down Cowflop Lane, to be penitent and get the half-day off.

Forty days after that it was Easter, even if it kept moving, and then forty days later, it was Ascension Day when we had to march down Cowflop Lane again, only we didn't have to be penitent this time because this was the happy day Jesus jumped off a hill like the gliders at Great Hucklow and flew off without an engine.

*

All Saints Church pretends to be 1066 with an apse and a rude screen. But it only really started in 1928 AD when Squire Somebody from Totley Hall paid for it to be built so that his name would never be forgotten.

When you joined the All Saints choir you were given the worst ruff that had been round every choirboy's tide-marked boily neck since Sexuagesima. And after your first Evensong you had to let yourself get Bushed at the back of the vestry.

My family didn't go to church.

Dad always said he'd help out with *Oliver to Cavalry* at Easter if they were short of tenors, but he never did. Mum didn't believe in God, and didn't believe she could sing, and women weren't allowed anyway. Our Geth had asthma. Our Dave turned Methodist.[54]

So it was just me.

I went alone to Matins and Evensong every Sunday, and to Choir every Thursday, never skiving off, for nine years. After I was confirmed, I went to Communion at 8 a.m. as well.

When I was 15, I was made a Server and I got a scarlet dress with eleven scarlet woolly buttons. I carried the cross, rang the bell and snuffed the candles. Everyone said I looked the part.

*

---

54 Yet years later Geth became both an enthusiastic Anglican and chorister.

The hymns were Ancient and Modern (Revised) but we didn't know what they meant when we sang them, e.g.

> *Forty days and forty nights*
> *Thou wast fasting in the wild;*
> *Forty days and forty nights*
> *Tempted, and yet undefiled.*

What's undefiled? And what's with wast? And why wast God allowed to thee and thou, when we got told off at school for it?

Some hymns were easy, because they were just sad -

> *Our blest Reindeer ere he breathed*
> *His tender last farewell*

Some were just mad, and it should have been beautiful anyway -

> *How beauteous are their feet*
> *Who stand on Zion's hill!*

Some made you dizzy when you tried to make out what they meant -

> *Cherubim and seraphim falling down before thee,*
> *Which wert, and art, and evermore shalt be.*

You sometimes had to help Jesus -

> *Should not we thy sorrow share*
> *And from worldly joys[55] abstain*
> *Fasting with unceasing prayer,*
> *Strong with thee to suffer pain?*

But what's the point of unceasing prayer and fasting and pain? God wasn't up in heaven listening to it when Jesus suffered pain, because He *was* Jesus, because that's what the Trinity means. He was His own Son. And after, he was His own Holy Ghost as well.

And He was the one who chose to suffer pain to save us. If He didn't like it, why didn't He choose some other way He did like, if He was reckoned to be God? And why could He have a capital letter all the time even when He wasn't starting a sentence?

---

55 And was 'worldly joy' Joy Frith, Julie Frith's older sister from the Community Centre?

I don't think I ever believed one ancient and modern word of it.[56]

*

Church was boring too, unless you were a Vicar.[57]

Nothing ever happened.

Choirboys weren't allowed to do anything between hymns and psalms except sit without crossing our legs, and wonder about why psalms had an extra p.

And wonder what Trinity meant in all those months of Sundays after it, before you got anyway near Advent and why even when you did it was ages till Christmas and why once you were there you were straight into Epiphany.

We also wondered if Vicars' daughters had to be virgins.

We memorised the Table of Affinity from The Book of Common Prayer and worked out how you couldn't marry your grandmother.[58] And pointed at Sexuagesima to make the probationary choirboys giggle.

We wondered how to spell Apopcprypha (not like that).

And puzzled about who built churches such daft shapes that you couldn't see things? And who got rude on which side of the rude screen?

I worried if, if my family, especially my Mum weren't going to be allowed to go to heaven, would I still have to? Just because I was in the choir?

And why did we always pray for the Royal Family first?

And why was Our Dave allowed to kiss the girls who smoked outside the Methodist youth club and could take down the smoke, when we Anglicans only had the Vicar's daughter who sat with her mother twice every Sunday, on the bridegroom's side, on an empty row in the empty church, and never quite smiled even when I was a badge boy?

---

56 But I heard Billy Graham at the Victoria Hall on a radio link when I was 14, and I got up out of my seat when he asked, and got born again. I did believe some of that, but not for long, thank God.

57 I played at being the vicar in our kitchen using the electric stove as the altar. I wore a tea towel as an academic hood, and my Mum and Dad sat smiling on the kitchen chairs. I said I was going to be a bishop when I grew up and then they'd be sorry for smiling.

58 Who'd want to? Even Grandy Chandler?

The Vicar's daughter and I met in London ages after and we did smile, but we were too ashamed of each other to do anything else.

Her father baptised me at 14 and I felt daft.

The Lord Bishop of Derby confirmed me the week after, and I felt nothing.

I stopped going to All Saints at 17, and nobody came round to 6 Laverdene Drive to ask if I'd died, even if dying was supposed to be the whole point.

Even on Your iPhone

6 Laverdene is in New Totley.

No one calls it that, but it's what the maps say it is, even on your iPhone.

Here, once, were great green oak forests with turnpikes and inns.

Then the oaks were cleared, and a great Victorian Pleasure Garden decreed, with boating lakes, bandstands, tennis courts and Jerome K. Jerome courting couples with moustaches, parasols and striped blazers, all riding on penny-farthings, and giggling at menageries of monkeys.

> *There I met a monkey*
> *Just like me!*

After the Victoria Pleasure Gardens went bust, there were market gardens and vast squeaking prairies of rhubarb.

Then the land was replanted with homes not quite fit for heroes, after the Great War that the Dore soldier and my Dad the Totley sailor had won for us. All that now grew in the monkey and rhubarb fields were builders' bottoms.

Up went the Green Oak and Aldam estates, miniature Parson Crosses on the edges of Derbyshire.

Up went the wobbly seaside houses of the Grove, all the way out to the beaches of Blackamoor.

Up went the Bayko Marstones, Stonecrofts, Rowan Tree Dells and Sunny Vales.

And up went the Laverdene, in five cul de sacs of boxed redbrick houses all identical then, and all different now.

In flooded hundreds of Yorkshire immigrants, pushing back the boundaries, interbreeding, and birthing the New Totley, full of common people.

Except For This One

I spent last August writing stuff for the annual competition run by the Poetry Business, just off Snig Hill. I wrote about all our childhoods, and our Dad in his Masonic regalia, and the meeting in our front room when the TOADS started, and the sexy number six, and the rhubarb fields squeaking above the monkeys, and about the night Dad died, taken from my Mum's diary. I wrote about the neighbours and first girl friends, and what happens when your family scatters.

I sent the poems off and waited to be turned into a Poetry Pamphlet and get invited to address roomsful of poets, with free beer.

When I didn't even get a mensh, I deleted my poems and stopped being a poet.

Except for this one, about growing up round Laverdene, without the mucky bit that was put in to get the judge's[59] attention.

Read it out loud, I would, but not too loud. And see if you can spot where I changed the mucky bit.

Common People

Ginger jams, tinned hams
furry slippers, kippers
calling the kids nippers

it's common too to
wear clothes that always smell of stew to
go to someone else's house to do your number two
to smell of onions, talk about your bunions
have your milk bottle
on your table

tomato sausages are common, let's agree,
so are brown sauce, haslet, bags and tripes
smoking other people's pipes,
wearing corduroy that smells of wee
or smelling of wee generally
or having more than two sugars in your tea
or having more than three

---

59 I'm not all that keen on the judge Andrew Motion's poetry, especially the one on the side of Hallam Uni.

kids to mither
and no twins neither
and not neither
like breather
neither

no saying pardon,
stripping off in the garden
being Irish or Scot
using the chest of drawers drawer instead of a cot
carrying round warm hankies squelching with snot

no pink jelly, baked beans
big telly, black jeans
stains
women's things blocking drains
no nits
motor bikes in the front room in bits
washing your hands on the tea towels

discussing your bowels
tide marks on dirty necks
or changing sex
segs
mottled legs
pink rugs around the lav
asking the milkman in, we know you have

no ferrets, berets
mispronouncing
coal, coil
school, skoil
letting your bosoms go round bouncing

don't have two dogs or more
barrybucknell your door
or your pelmet
no crash helmet

chips
cold-sored lips
freckles
spectacles
drop handle bicycles
tip top
spion kop

caged birds in the kitchen
impetigo, general itching
stocking tops, hygienic shops

park drives, second wives
keeping your dog in a kennel

heavy petting up the jennel
spaghetti in a tin

putting stuff in next door's bin
using the soubriquet Aunty for your aunts

sleeping in your pants
don't think we'll be impressed

if you shave in your vest
use brylcreem, durex, preparation x
say sex

keep pigeons in the back
get the sack
show your crack
shave downstairs
wear flares

play drums to disrupt us
offer sweets to corrupt us
keep us awake with coitus

interruptus
don't do favours
or first name neighbours.
your front door's for the undertaker
come to take you to your maker.

To be no better than you should be is common
and not uncommon
and a shame. [60]

---

60 A published poet said not to include the last three lines. I do wonder now if they say the opposite of what I think I meant them to mean.

3. I Should Like To See You Enjoy This Egg

Enter 1952
All that survives of my diary of 1952.

Tues 1st Jan
Today we got up very late and I gave an Archie A[61] Show. We went to Nanny Robbo's in afternoon. Bury beat Utd 1-0.

Wed 2nd Jan
Today we went to Nanny's for dinner. Paul and Mary were there. Geth went home early to hear his tunes. In Podge's Newfooty[62] Cup Utd 1 Wed 2.

Thur 3rd Jan
Today Mummy started painting and Hewson Fawcett came. I fewsed the radiator by touching the bar with wire. Got a puzzle and went to choir.

Fri 4th Jan
Got up late. Mother had still to finish painting and today Geth helped her. Went to pictures with Needhams in afternoon.

Sat 5th Jan
This morning I published the Blacklands Gazette. Sheff United played Wednesday and Wednesday lost at home 3-1, the 2nd win for Utd this season.

Sun 6th Jan
Went to Church twice in choir.

Mon 7th Jan
Last day at home. Played Podge at Newfooty and I lost 5-1. Daddy got library ticket.

Tues 8th Jan
Got up early and went back to school. Stuart Shepherd was not at school. Got 54-55 for English. Rodney came and we played at Newfooty. He won 2-1.

Wed 9th Jan
Got up early, went to school. We had drawing at Mrs Cawoods in the hall. Went to Cubs and Cub party is on Sat.

Thur 10th Jan
Got up early, went to school. Went to choir practice at night. Bed rather late.

Fri 11th Jan
Got up early went to school.

---

61 Archie Andrews was a radio ventriloquist's puppet. Mine had a mouth that flapped up and down and a head that swivelled. His shoes kept falling off. It was entertainment but not as we know it.
62 Newfooty was Subutteo-lite, the Betamax of table football. The players kept falling over, and the goalie got stuck in his netting. But it was better than blow football because that made you faint.

Folks!

Seriously, if you bought this book hoping it might have more famous people in it than it seems to have had so far, hold tight, and wait till when you can be really famous with me and my son Goronwy[63] in Deptford in 1981.

---

63 He's since met Eddie Izzard, sailed the Atlantic with John Humphreys, met Lembik Opik and kissed Esther Ranzen goodnight, off Gib. But even all these put together aren't as famous as we were in 1981.

First words

In a black foolscap hardback notebook, borrowed from the Dad's Town Hall, with a sticky label on the front saying *Story Scraps* compiled by JGR and in various colours and handwritings and noms de plumes, I launched my writing career, with *John's Unwilling Trip* (1951).

> *John's aunt had said he could go where he liked while she saw his uncle off. John said he would go to the cliffs and he took sandwiches and started out. It was a sunny day but the landlady Mrs O Donnelly told him that it would cloud over and soon rain. John however took no notice and left without a coat.*

Then there is *They Called Me a Coward*, a short story set in 1940 in which Richard Johnson tries to join up, but has to become a reporter on the *Star* instead.

Then there is Detective Mottram that begins -

> *'Listen to this!' exclaimed Detective Inspector Curtis, 'Josiah Kingsley is dead!'*

Next is *Wilkins and Mr Campbell* that begins, with the correct punctuation -

> *"'A queer chap he was, wearing a big bowler and he said 'Don't bother me my lad' when I asked him the time."*

The stories merge into each other and into unfinished songs in C major, and home-made miniature newspapers, and annotated moves from telephone chess games, and the latest scores from Newfooty on our kitchen table.[64]

> *Big Bill Tempest sat blowing his hands impatiently. He was sitting in the snack room of the Daily Star of which he was a reporter. He stood up as his fiancé Kitty Webster came in. She was also a reporter on the Star and the two had a reputation of being the duo at reporting. Kitty was, although she didn't know it the daughter of the editor. She had been injured during the war and had lost her memory.*

---

64 Helen Creswell the children's writer told us at a Chesterfield literary festival that you can tell the kids who'll be writers when they grow up, not from any quality in what they write as kids, but from how fascinated they are by ink, paper, carbons, desks, blotting paper, typewriters, tippex, rubbers, sharpeners pencils, biros, nibs, felt tips, and rulers. With me it's pads. Still.

My first surviving play, *An Intractable Case*, features a Physician, a Patient and a Maid.

> **PHYSICIAN**
> Normal. And now we must build up your strength. Let me see. Yes I have it. You will have you one lightly boiled egg.
>
> **PATIENT**
> Thanks. I may have one later on. I couldn't face it now.
>
> **PHYSICIAN**
> Tut. You must fight this Post Influenza Depression. Come I should like to see you enjoying this egg before I go.
>
> **PATIENT**
> You can't I'm afraid. Louis is out of the flat.
>
> **PHYSICIAN (with great gusto)**
> Then I will boil you one myself.

Later there are notes for a long book about my Form 2(1) at King Edward's, to feature chapters on each of the following boys -

Andrew Averill Beckett Beckman Brooksbank Cartwright Cash Cliff Crank Darwin Ellis Gibson Gordon Goulden Jones Linstead McNaught Morton Mosley O' Shea Readman Rigby Robinson Roddis Sheriff Stokes Topham Wagstaff Worswick and Yates.[65]

---

65 Two of them became knights.
At least one died of drink.
One said he never masturbated.
One became a top Doctor. One a top Astronomer.
There were several professors, and one judge.
Two lived in Spain avoiding each other.
Two were successful writers.
At least two of them at least kissed at least two others of them's sisters.
One was nicknamed Minnie for being small, and one Piggy for being fat and one Stodge for being McNaught.
One was supposed to have died but hadn't.
I was best man at two of their weddings.
I sat in front of one in the Lyceum stalls last year and asked about his banjo.
One of them wore belt, braces and boots and was humiliated by the teachers for being common but became a successful town hall wallah and I interviewed him once.
One had a glass eye he used to suck. One had private parts to die for.

Fists, Feet, Chalk and Board Rubbers

In 1995, for their 90th anniversary, Peter Lawton edited a collection of King Edward VII School pupils' memories.

He called it *Tha'll Never Get In Thear* and he asked me to submit a paragraph.

The other contributors are kinder than me and if it's charity you want, read the whole book on the KES alumni website.

I'm a bit surprised by my own screechiness, now. But I am impressed - I was then - that Peter printed it, uncensored.

I said I thought King Edward's was one of the most disturbed and disturbing establishments I'd ever been in -

> *I was yelled at in the vestibule on my very first morning while we were still queuing to get in, and I was yelled at in the vestibule on the very last afternoon when I was trying to say goodbye and get out.*

> *There was so much yelling.*

> *And hitting, of course, with canes and rulers and slippers and fists and feet and chalk and board rubbers.*

I discussed the King Edward's pecking orders -

> *Oxford was better than Cambridge, just, and Cambridge was much better than Durham, which was better than London.*

> *Greek was best, then Latin, which was better than French which was better than German which was better than Spanish which was easy.*

> *Arts were better than Sciences, but Art itself was only better than Woodwork.*

> *Biology was for girls.*

> *Girls didn't matter except that they could get pregnant and stop you getting to Oxford.*

I deconstructed the necrophilia -

Old and dead was always best.

Yet my King Edward's itself was just a muddle of made-up Greek declamations, sporting blues, honours boards, houses, initiations, surnames, beatings, prefects, sub-prefects, and smug teaching about things that were valued most highly only when they were most useless.

I analysed the staff -

Most of the teachers were shabby bullies.

All of them went in humiliating daily fear of the dreadful Headmaster, N L Clapton, who jeered and snarled his fat way through their lives as much as through ours. They were grimly cynical about their subjects, dictating and boring straight from their textbooks.

They set us endless memorising homeworks to occupy every night for seven years so we didn't join youth clubs or talk to our parents.

I mused on the politics -

They were all Tories of course, living in fear of the working-class of Sheffield who paid their wages. That was why we were caned for not wearing our caps on the buses or for eating in the street.

They were usually racists too. One Geography teacher started every lesson, as he shut the curtains for another epidiascope tour of African huts while we played with our trousers, 'Right, let's see how the wogs are getting on.'

And I concluded -

There was no creativity at my King Edward's, only twitchy classical music, essays and translations. What there was instead was that particular nastiness that you find in all-male establishments when everyone's desperate not to let on that they do sometimes love and care for each other in spite of everything. And we did.

Some of the friends and lovers I had in that Broomhill concentration camp are dear friends still, forty years on.

In spite of the relentless competitiveness, and dark sarcasm from the teachers, we actually laughed a lot (they didn't like that).

We did help each other, and we didn't let the buggers win.

We taught ourselves things they never knew about as we tossed our way together in and out of puberty. It was a small triumph of the human spirit - and just about the only consolation I can find in my King Edward's story, then or now.

So, a fairly balanced account then.

After that book came out, my daughters Eleanor and Megan went to King Ted's (by then a mixed Comp) for their Sixth Form. They laughed and made music and had art exhibitions in my Hall. When Eleanor was awarded a psychology prize, I sat in the very seat in the balcony where I'd been sitting forty years before so I could call out at the performers, as scripted, in the Staff Review, only to be hoiked off by the deputy head and yelled at in front of my own parents.

Good week
**One Week in September, when I am 16, as recorded in my Boots
Scribbling Diary - British manufacture throughout.**

On Sunday I must -

> *polish my thoughts*

and -

> *put on the style.*

On Monday I see the Headmaster because I've realised half way through
the two-year course that I've got a hopeless mixture of A level subjects -
Economics, English and French - and need to swap History for French. I give
a speech at the International Discussion Group in the school library and

> *impress favourably.*

And -

> *I have won the scripture prize, I am surprised to learn.*

On Tuesday -

> *It is done. I am now a specialist in history.*[66]

With A level coming up in 9 months -

> *I can probably do it with a lot of work.*

On Wednesday I enter school with Rodney[67] -

> *for the first time since infant schooldays doing different subjects. We
> have always done exactly the same subjects in exactly the same
> sets for something like 11 years.*

---

66 History chaps, geography maps.
67 Rod Andrew, of Janet and Rodney. His Aunty Sally was my All Sainted Old Ma Peacock.
He wasn't allowed to say that though, except to me. He was my best friend and a skilled
footballer, and lived on Laverdene Close next-but-one to where my niece Steph and her Eric
now are. We've never met on purpose since but when by chance we do, he still chuckles, and
looks bemused, and we buy each other drinks.

And -

history will not be easy.

On Thursday -

I shall get the economics prize this year, which pleases me immensely.

On Friday I have to sign the Late Book -

and see Carter after dinner...and the irony of the situation is that I was the prefect on late duty.

On Saturday a pal tells me -

about a book in the library in which is a man's thoughts for the entire day, written down. The book is very large, much of the material being at worst 'burnable'. The idea is good I feel. One could write an entire book in a day that way...if ever I find myself in a spot for a plot I might try this scheme - but what a pity this author[68] thought of it before this diarist.[69]

---

68 James Joyce?
69 Me

4. A Phase He's Going Through

Going to Work

It was the hot summer of Christine Keeler.[70]

I'd left school and got work as a clerk in the Water Department at the Town Hall. My job was to re-register and de-register the taps, hosepipes and WCs that had been registered or de-registered at the counter and brought to us on white cards. We wrote the details in ledgers that were then sent down to Rating.

Among the eight other men at our long table were two who did leaks, and a one who was matrimonially-challenged and went out in his raincoat all the hot summer of Christine Keeler, looking for unregistered taps, hosepipes and WCs.

There were five other long tables of men, and a sprinkling of pretty girls who never looked at me in my £6 suit (almost exactly what the pay was per week, paid per month) except on Saturday mornings when I could wear my sports jacket.

I had become a Town Hall wallah like my Dad.

He and I ate ham and mustard sandwiches three times a week at lunchtimes in the Peace Gardens all hot summer, and I read up on the Profumo scandal in The Daily Telegraph. He arranged, via the Masons I think, that I could have a three hour lunch hour twice a week so we could dive into The Wadsley Jack and have a glass of ginger beer shandy on the way to Nanny Robbo's in Hillsborough, for lamb dinner, milk pudding, tea and a nap.

The wallahs were nice enough but …

Working as a labourer on previous summers, I'd got brown, and fit, and learned about swearing and skiving, and enjoyed laughing comradeships against foremen and passing ratepayers who thought we weren't working hard enough.

We wallahs were white and dusty and didn't laugh or swear or enjoy ourselves at all.

*

---

70 She was a Tory sex scandal, famous for straddling a chair backwards, naked.

Ten years later I wrote two plays about a matrimonially-challenged man who counted water at the dusty white Town Hall in the Summer of Christine Keeler.[71]

And twenty years later, Christine Keeler herself turned up in Reception at Radio Sheffield. She was very small, older and alone, sitting on a chair the proper way round. I said hello and she smiled. I could see what the fuss had been about. I shook her hand, which was small and warm.

---

71 I googled her when writing this, and found that I am remembering her wrong by two years.

Going Up

In January 1959, by train on my own for the first time, I'd gone from Sheffield Victoria to Oxford, and come back three days later with a hundred pound Open Stock Scholarship in Modern History at Keble College.

Being a Scholar, and the Senior Scholar too, meant that when I Went Up in Michaelmas term, I'd have to have three windows in my rooms, wear a long gown, sit on the Scholars' table at dinner in Hall, lead Grace in Latin -

> *Miserere nostri te quisomethingmus*

- and promise not to get married.

*

On my first afternoon at Keble I was crossing the Sunken Quad under clouds of Etonian braying, pretending I wasn't there, and I met this Aston Villa-Labour-supporting, train-crash enthusing, smoking son of a car worker from Birmingham, and he became Little Max Johnson, my first Oxford lifetime friend.

We then met the next one, Little Rafe Paine.

And then Little Alan and some other Davises and Davieses including Tony who said he'd pray for me, and Walford who said he came from Wales.[72]

We were all grammar school boys, and, not so terrified together, off we strolled to the Broad to buy our long red white and black Keble scarves to post back to our Mums for them to stitch on our Cash's name tags, so we would know who we were whenever we got lost for the rest of our lives.

*

Keble is, by Oxford standards, a new college. It was designed in Victorian red brick for the poor sons of poor clergy. The architecture avoids the usual sin-sodden Oxford staircases, where floppy blond Bullingdon toffs lounge on sofas by real coal fires with burgundy wine, and play with teddy bears. Our Rooms were small cells and came on long prison corridors, with little electric bars. Sofas were forbidden. We had just a small table, an empty bookcase,

---

72 Who became one of the two Walford Davieses who remember more about Dylan Thomas than Dylan Thomas ever did.

a squeaky single bed, and a washstand with a basin for the shaving water we never needed, which the servant brought in regardless, saying, each morning -

Quarter to eight sir?

- whatever time it was.

We each had an *Oak*. That was an extra door that you could sport in front of your real door when you were doing anything you wanted to hide.

The St Pancras *Chapel* had a little windowless room on its right where there was supposed to be this famous painting by Holman Hunt of Jesus holding a lantern at a door in a garden, and looking sad in His crown of thorns. You couldn't see if He was Him because of the dark but if He was, He was *The Light of the World*.

There was a Gothic *Clocktower* with a gold clock that tinned out the quarter hours, and a Gothic Library full of the icy busts of unmarried vicars.

We boys were called *men*. The servants were called *scouts* and they had to make your bed, wash your pots, report you to the Warden if you tried to go home in term-time, and call you sir whether you liked it or not.

Mrs B. was the college's only female scout. She ran the only Keble staircase, which was the *Clocktower*. We migrated to her as soon as we could, because she was Annie Bottomley from Sheffield, chuckly, bosomy and about 40, with no children of her own. She brought us thick brown tea in bed, and you could taste the Henderson's. She lent us cigarettes and said we could pay her back when we'd grown up.

There was a *Beer Cellar* with a dartboard where we played *Keble*[73] before Dinner in our gowns, and we had to start by saying *middlefordiddle*.

There was a *Buttery* to buy stuff on *Battels*.

There was a *JCR* where we could make suggestions in the Suggestions Book, and steal the Keble-crested notepaper to impress our mums when we sent them our weekly parcel of mucky laundry, sealed with red wax.

There was a *Porter's Lodge* with a vast door. After dinner we had to clamber in through a little door in the vast door. After midnight we had to climb in over

---

73 Everyone else calls it 'Killer'.

the bike sheds and hope to get caught just once for our memoirs.[74]

People at other colleges laughed at Keble.

But so did we - e.g. we sang about ourselves to the tune of Beethoven's Ninth -

> *Keble college architecture's*
> *Something quite fantastical!*
> *Something something something something*
> *Matters ecclesiastical!*
> *See the young aspiring bishops*
> *They never heard of actresses!*
> *Something something something something*
> *Homosexual practices!*

If you got *Sconced* at Dinner the scouts came round with eight pints of beer and you drank them all without taking your lips off the silver tureen they came in. To get sconced, you had to mention a woman's name. We didn't know any, so we left it to the Old Etonian boating lot. They didn't know any women either, but they liked being sick, and the rules didn't apply to them anyway. They also liked burning boats and standing in the fireplace of the *JCR* shouting about *grey men, grammar school trogs and oiks*. They took Fourths, became lawyers and weren't very clever

But most of Oxford wasn't very clever.

That's the most useful thing I learned there.

*

The only work we had to do was a *Tutorial* for one hour a week, when we had to read out our essay to a tutor as he bit his pipe in front of his real fire, or made lukewarm cocoa he'd borrowed from an undergraduate down the corridor. If it was after 11, or sometimes if it wasn't, he offered sherry instead.

In spite of this academic rigour, we still managed to get out to see Bergman films at the *Scala*, usually the *Seventh Seal*, and Pamela Green[75] films at the *Moulin Rouge* in Headington, especially *Naked as Nature Intended* that Max still likes though he has taken a less active interest in naturism since he married Chrissie.

---

74 Never was.
75 'Blonde pony-tailed retro glamour legend.' Her films usually tell of what happens to prudish girls who by mistake wander into nudist colonies in Norfolk, then take off their glasses, and clothes, to play table tennis.

We drank Morrell's beer and learned Bar Billiards.

We went to the Union, joined clubs, tried beards, punted, squashed, talked, bought books, sofas, bow ties, shortbread, lotions, spot potions, a typewriter, pipe racks and tobacco jars with crests. Rafe learned basic guitar. Alan ran fast.

In History we learned that religion caused Oliver Cromwell, or the other way round, and that there were no causes of the First World War.

*

And then we were history ourselves.

> *If you once start looking behind you*
> *And start retracing your steps*
> *Remind me to remind you*
> *We said we wouldn't look back.*

The salad days were over. Keble hadn't lasted long. We all got our second-class degrees. My tutor, a Welshman called Eric Stone and the only don I liked, and I thought liked me, wrote a goodbye letter -

> *Perhaps some day you would like to explain why your friend*
> *Goulden[76] got a First and you didn't. I have my own ideas on the*
> *subject.*

Right at the end we allowed our parents to come up as long as they promised to behave. We brought Mrs B. to meet them and we all had two sherries[77] and one last punt up the Cherwell.

Years later I was talking about Mrs B. on Radio Sheffield, saying how Oxford would have been tons harder without her, and how we'd love to meet her again and pay her back, now we were grown up.

A relative rang in to say she'd died that weekend.

---

76 Sir John Goulden formerly of the FO, formerly of 2(1) at King Edward's. His mother later went to Rotherham. She became a keen Radio Sheffield listener, and used to tell him what I'd been up to as he roamed the world being diplomatic. We met last year after her funeral and he told me he'd never told his own kids which way he voted, and was surprised I was surprised.
77 I've never drunk it since.

Gaol Bait

You were on 25ᵗʰ October 1961 convicted by this court and were ordered to pay a fine of £2 and 10/- cost within 28 days.
Marylebone Magistrates Court 25th Oct 1961[78]

---

78 Why though?

Going Down

Sitting in the Oxford Union[79] Library just after 3 p.m. on Sunday November 5th 1961, seven terms in, I hand-wrote my editorial for *Cherwell, The Oxford University Newspaper* and, at the stroke of a fountain pen, changed history.

Mine anyway.

> *This is another tasteless attack on the Monarchy and if that doesn't appeal to you, don't read on.*

I added, after a couple of paragraphs -

> *You may even like to read that the Duke Edinburgh does not wear pants under his kilt.*

*

When I'd finished, eight minutes and 500 words later, I took it round to the *Cherwell* office at the back of the Union Debating Hall, a one-storey survivor of the War, prefabby, asbestossy and long gone. It was always cold enough to keep your duffel coat on, even in Eights Week, even if you weren't posing.

I two-fingered my royalist editorial onto the *Imperial*, did the layout and chose the *ultra bodoni* headline, swapped news with my News team, and waited till the *Turfs, Turls, Birds, Bears* and *Lambs* opened for Sunday beer.

As soon as they did, we posted the features, photo blocks, wallpaper layouts and my royal editorial nobody had read but me, and off they went to the Witney Press to be hot-metalled in an old two-storey barnful of men in brown coats.

*

I loved playing at being a journalist on *Cherwell*, going to places I'd never dare, asking things I'd never dare, and typing it all up my own daring way after.

I loved the other *Cherwell* journalists who played with me too.

---

79 Three regrets about my lucky life. One, I went to an all boys' school. Two, I went bald too early. Three, I never spoke at the Oxford Union.

One ended up editing *The Guardian*, and one *The Times*.[80]

One went on to edit both *Reveille* and the *Daily Sport.*

One got knighted for services to Mrs Thatcher on the *Express* and *News of the World.*

Guardian theatre critic Michael Billington was our theatre man.

The Head of BBC Sport was on my staff, and I worked for the future editor of the future *Real Beer Guides.*

To say nothing of Sir Simon the Best Church, and Lord Melvyn the South Bank.

We all took patient turns at the *Imperial* and the phone, making up stories (which is why they are called *stories*) about the Bodleian Library falling down, or about another new plan to build another new road under Christ Church Meadows, under our own by-lines, for ever.

And I was going to be a journalist for ever too of course.

But -

*

In the previous week's *Cherwell* there were stories about new proposals to extend the Modern History syllabus to 1918, and the latest stage of *Cherwell's* campaign for women to be allowed to join the Oxford Union. *A Taste of Honey* was at the Ritz, a business lunch at the *Golden City* on Ship Street was four shillings, including pudding, and *Private Eye* was starting that week and was -

> *particularly keen to use new talent especially at Oxford.*

And I'd just written in my two-fingered editorial -

> *One has always had a sneaking suspicion that the sexy side of the royal family was its appeal, from Queen Caroline showing her magnificent breasts, to the cavorting of some very recent characters in high places.*

*

---

80 Tony Capstick, my double-heading broadcasting pal at Radio Sheffield always claimed his ideal job would be Editor of Health & Efficiency.

On the Monday after, I was cycling from my dingy digs in Headington, off to a tutorial at Christ Church about *Was There An Agrarian Revolution in the 1800s?*[81] and this journalist, who was a bit shabby even by my standards, came out of a hedge backwards and showed me his press cutting from that morning's *Daily Telegraph*. There was this *Row Over Sex and Royalty Editor*, he said, and I was about to be *Sent Down from Oxford*, so did I agree with ALP Norrington the Vice Chancellor saying I was -

> *stupid and offensive?*

And did I also realise that yesterday -

> *The Proctors were studying a copy of the newspaper published at the weekend as part of their normal duties under which they see all undergraduate publications as they are printed?*

And that -

> *Only one reader supported Mr Robinson?*

*

Now, I'd made up this kind of story myself, on becalmed *Cherwell* afternoons.

Someone says something. You put them in inverted commas saying it, more or less. You include their age and marital status. You've got your quote.

Now ring somebody who'll disagree, read them your quote and check their age and marital status. Put what they more or less say in inverted commas. You've now got your row.

Ring somebody more or less in charge and ask what they are doing about the row. Put them in inverted commas etc. and you've got your *story*.

Then make it one sentence per paragraph, sub it and sex it up and put in with what we journalists call crossheads, which are exciting words you pinch from the story itself to keep the reader reading, like -

SEXY

And then you've got your sexy story.

---

81 It depends on what you mean by 'Agrarian', 'Revolution', and the '1800s'.

The journalist who'd got mine nodded when I explained my principled beliefs about the place of a monarchy in a modern democracy, and asked if I'd got a fiancée.

I said I'd got a tute, on the Agrarian Revolution, if there was one, so goodbye. And off I cycled to Christ Church.

I felt pleased. Fancy anyone taking any notice of anything you ever write.

His stories made the national and local papers for days.

I got too many letters and phone calls.

I stopped being quite so pleased.

DONE IT

The Cherwell news staff went on making up next week's stories (but didn't include mine). Nobody suggested starting a petition about an imminent threat to free speech. Or me. No one even said I was an idiot.

We ignored our own story, and waited.

My pals at Keble crossed the sunken quad in their bumfreezer gowns and said -

>   *He's done it now Rafe, yah?*
>   *Yah Alan. Middle for diddle?*

- and went to the beer cellar to talk about where to do their teacher training next year.

My tutor shrugged at me in the Sunken Quad.

LOVE

My Mum wrote -

>   *Dear John,*
>
>   *Daddy's just had a phone call from the Daily Express - in London! - who asked Daddy's views on your writings in Cherwell re the Royal family and Daddy replied that he has always encouraged you to write*

openly and express your opinion - though these might not always be the same as his!

Don't get yourself too involved however! It's not worth upsetting your Oxford Life.

Lots of love, Mum.

Then there was a PS[82] from Dad -

Following your call tonight.

Don't worry John - I'll see you through.

We all make mistakes and don't worry about the press reports. Star report enclosed.

Love Dad.

Dad was quoted in the papers saying -

It's just a phase he's going through

- which is the worst thing he ever did to me.[83] He hadn't seen a copy of my editorial, so he'd no idea what I'd written anyway. Nobody had.[84]

RUINED

And I, martyred and waiting for something to happen, wished as always that I'd written more carefully, especially if this is what I was going to be remembered for at Oxford for ever, like Shelley.[85]

More Fleet Street came round.

---

82 And the longest letter my Dad ever wrote me.
83 My daughter Eleanor read this and pointed out that the paper probably made it up anyway. My daughter Megan read it and said wasn't I angry with my Dad?
84 There was a second anti-royal editorial. I never knew which one I got the bollocking for.
85 Anti-royal atheist writer P. B. Shelley, who wouldn't recant even when his dad said he had to, so he got sent down from Oxford in 1811. His Skylark is the only poem I know off by heart, only I don't.

And so did David Frost from *Associated Rediffusion TV*, who bought my first ever gin and tonic, and a fish lunch at the poshest restaurant in Oxford. He was on the phone all the time, and went back to London without finishing his *bouillabaisse.*

The *Daily Express* filled me with beer and took me to an Action Painting Party in North Oxford, and I ruined my duffle coat for the next five years by falling into an action-painted wall.

BEHIND THE BUSHES

I asked photographers not take my photo, and they agreed not to, then did, from behind the bushes.

The Proctors, whose job is to punish undergraduates who bring the good name of their University into disrepute, went on studying their copy of *Cherwell* till the end of the following week. They then summonsed me, in *sub fusc*, which is the serious Oxford fancy dress of cap, gown, black suit,[86] white bow tie, and black socks.

They kept me imprisoned in the Sheldonian for ages.

YES!

Then -

> *Vade mecum! Doff mortarboards. Salve!*

> *Salve!!!*

> *Did I acknowledge I was in statu pupillarii?*

> *I agree!*

> *Had I inter alia written pro rata something ad hoc?*

---

86 Max Johnson tells me in a phone call - I had no trousers to wear. Dick Yarrow a Maths ex-national service undergraduate, and a man with immense enthusiasm for sexual intercourse, in theory, and who was later Mrs Thatcher's agent at Finchley, got some brown paper and ironed some trousers for me. I then stood with my back to Max's fire and burned a hole in the bottom. Max stuck it together with Sellotape. It might have happened like that. I don't remember. But when I told him about the petition he signed a few days later he didn't remember that. I told him, 'We're all historians now - we remember only what helps us to half-understand the past.'

Yes!

Did I plan obiter dicta per se more?

No never.

Did I pari passu pro bono wish to?

Yes please!

Had I been a mutatis mutandis at all?

Oh yes. No rather.

No more about it then yah? Well causus bellum and goodnight. Doff and vale.

Yes. Thank you.

I rang home, even if it wasn't Sunday, and my Mum and I cried[87].

SEX

Meg - Sexy? The student editor of a college newspaper was getting angry letters today because he wrote that one of Princess Margaret's chief appeals was sex. From Princess Margaret's spokesman: 'No comment.'
The San Francisco Examiner, November 14th 1961.

BOSOMS

The same weekend, however, that I'd been teasing dead Queen Caroline about her bosoms, I'd received this letter -

---

87 My Mum, being a lifelong socialist and atheist had nil respect for the monarchy. After she died, the TOADS of Totley got involved in a controversy about whether they should continue to play the National Anthem at the start of every play they did, to quieten the audience. My Mum's enthusiasm for the National Anthem was one of the key things that makes the TOADS keep playing God Save the King to this day. My Mum, wherever she isn't, will be laughing, as she always was.

St Hilda's
Oxford.

November 8th

Dear Rony,

I think you might be able to use the following: -

On Friday November 3rd a First Year at St Hilda's was ill in bed. Her boy friend came round to visit her in the afternoon and was found in bed with her at 4.30pm by a scout bringing in tea. The matter was reported and the girl immediately sent down. The man in question has been rusticated by his college for two weeks.

The girl's punishment apparently comes under rule 14 of College Rules - any member of college in statu pupilari whose residence is in the opinion of the Governing Body no longer desirable may be required to go down.

By the way don't use my name - I've been running too many troublesome petitions of late for my safety in the college to be all that certain.

I think I passed it to News.

Then I got another summons from the Proctors - no no, not a summons this time. Of course not, no. But if they could just meet me somewhere, please? At my convenience? Without all the sub fusc nonsense? Informal chat? Give them some advice? Yah?

*

And meanwhile this rapidly-cobbled, innumerate petition had begun to circulate -

TO THE VICE CHANCELLOR, THE PROCTORS, ALL HEADS OF COLLEGES AND SCRS

To avoid friction in the future between senior and junior members of the University we suggest that the following principles be commonly recognised (while granting that individual discretion may need to be applied). That:

The private sexual behaviour of a junior member of the University is primarily his or her own responsibility. College authorities should penalise only when they can claim to have a secondary responsibility, which arises in two cases:

(1) When the moral reputation of the institution in their charge would be seriously damaged.
(2) When a junior member's sexual behaviour amounts to a persistent imposition upon the freedom and welfare of others.
(3) In no circumstances should college authorities punish solely for disregard of conventional morality.

It was signed by the Union President, the *Isis* editor, the Labour, Liberal and Conservative Presidents and Chairmen, all the undergraduate big wigs – and by Max Johnson Pres Education Socy.[88]

Not by me, though.

I was with the Proctors -

Most kind. Come in do. Coffee at all? Sherry even? Give the Proctors some advice? Appreciated! Time's changing? Finger on the pulse? Did I think it might be good on balance not to give any more publicity to the two St Hilda's chaps in bed? Help them not bring themselves into disrepute yah? No more about it? Yah? Top you up?

Maybe *Cherwell* could have helped.[89]

But we didn't.

*

Cherwell never ran the story of the St Hilda's couple.

Or of the petition.

We never ran any account of the *sub fusc* attack on free speech.

Or of the secret censorship over the sherry.

---

88 !
89 Fifty years later, over lunch at another university, I learned what happened after, and I don't think it would have made any difference - to them - anyway.

We never even ran the story of me, *the sex and royalty editor.*

My lifetime's five best scoops ever, in one week.

And I'd met some real journalists too.

I decided I shouldn't be one myself after all.

I'd train to be a teacher like all the other grammar school oiks and grey men at Keble. Maybe run the school magazine and try not to get into trouble with that?[90]

---

90 I did. And did.

5. Not Before Time We Did

Greenwich Meantimes

When Oxford graduates were interviewed for the Oxford Department of Education for the *Dip. Ed.* course, the Director sometimes asked –

> *Do you like boys?*

I sort of shrugged when he asked me, because I thought it might be a trick question. I didn't know any boys anyway. And I couldn't say that I only wanted to train to be a teacher in Oxford at all because of *Cherwell* and Max.

But ten years later, I knew that tricky Oxford question was probably the only question teachers ever need to ask, or be asked.

> *Do you like kids?*

I'd even say you have to love them, really, to be a decent teacher.

*

Anyway, having done my extra year's Oxford training in how to teach History in a leafy boys' public school, I got a job teaching English in a huge mixed London comprehensive.

I found I did like boys. And girls. And teachers. I fell in love all over the place, back in a normal environment, ten years too late.

And I knew from my first September day there that I was going to teach for ever, probably here in England's biggest comprehensive, Eltham Green School, with its five gyms, library on its roof, its kids' art all over the building, its own theatre and, for all the humiliations, all its laughs.

*

In the second year, I rented a semi in Earshall Road SE9, and founded the prototype of our teachers' communes.

Not much of a prototype. More four teachers living together with a kitty for food, and never quite enough rooms or lav paper.

Earlshall Road SE9 was a very old man's house, with gardenfuls of soft fruit. The nearest pub was the *Wellcome*, which was not welcoming, and nowhere near, down two identical miles of Eltham.

Living with me here now were Alan Davis the Oxford runner, teaching history in Kent, Alan O'Shea from Sheffield, teaching English at the new comprehensive up the road, and Dave Wasp from Southampton and Keble, now teaching History at my school.

They were all in their first year, so not much company. I started a novel about us, cooked roast dinners on Sundays, got BBC 2 for *The Likely Lads* and Bob Dylan, and bought a ukulele.

George Hill[91] who already taught French at Eltham Green came round on Friday evenings to sing *San Francisco Bay,* if we didn't go out first.

We had some cramped parties with *Red Barrel* and soft fruit.

When the very old man died, the lettings agency sent us to a dark villa in Lewisham SE6 where we were burgled, and had parties with cheese and pineapple. For a treat, some Fridays we trekked over Blackheath to *The Green Man* to see a man play the musical saw.

The times were a-changing though.

It was at Lewisham that one of the Alans surprisingly needed condoms early one Sunday morning. And an illegal immigrant moved in and slept for several months on a marble slab in our darkened attic.

When we were turned out, Alan Davis went to live over a greengrocer with George and the guitar. And we went on to found *The Maze Hill Commune (1966-69)*.

*

Well, not so much a commune.

More a grimy, tiny, between-the-wars brick semi with two bare lawns, a garage, no attic or cellar, a cupboard kitchen, two small bedrooms, one very small bedroom, a lav without a door, and a sour bathroom. And all on a fast main road.

---

91 Westmoreland and Pot Hall, he is now George Hill the folk singer, often at the Rock at Maltby, and a late-onset songwriter, with a masterpiece about a man who tries to erect a flat-pack wardrobe. Carolyn his wife taught D. H. Lawrence two doors down from me in London, and is now an artist. Their daughter Catherine shares my birthday and my daughter Megan shares George's. And we all think their Jonathan's lovely.

But we were opposite Greenwich Park, a minute-and-a-quarter from the *Plume of Feathers.* Between us we could just afford Mrs Weaver to be our cleaner. We could watch the World Cup, listen to Sgt Pepper, and wait for girls.

Malcolm[92] scalped himself on a tree when we were making an 8mm French film, to impress some girls on a Sunday afternoon. And it was here at the Maze Hill Commune that we all enjoyed a 1968 situationist joke that involved unscrewing the lavatory door, and replacing it with a blanket.

We had parties with wine boxes. We laughed at the runners and riders in the Maze Hill Stakes, who were the identical people, in the identical order who passed our front window every weekday morning on their way to the station to be important in the City, proving daily the casual brutality of capitalism.

We were only a tunnel away from *The Iron Bridge* in the East End where they had a dirty comic called Geoff who told the same topical joke every Saturday about a man whose car broke down on the M1. There was also a bloke who sang *Your Cheating Heart,* and shouldn't have. Brian Epstein was usually in the audience, and some Krays.

We plodged round Greenwich Park in the snow, and straddled the Time Signal when relatives called, and looked for courting couples in the season.

We went to the theatre on Fridays, and had Instant Whip at porky Sunday lunches. On Tuesdays in the *Plume* we became the *NBGs,* and took on ladies darts teams, and Spud and Dusty.

I repainted the front room jonquil one Saturday lunchtime. Friends came over to admire it and to squeak in the red rexine suite, and play *Risk.*

I sang in the mornings in the bath, DJing The Alan Show, which was a pirate radio station using a Dansette with a lid that could be separated from the deck and pushed into early bedrooms.

> *Wake up early in the morning*
> *Hear the birdies say good morning*
> *The way the birdies said good morning*
> *When the birdies said good morning*
> *In my Ohio home.*

---

92 Malcolm Kisby, the illegal on the slab. Leicester, Newcastle Uni. Beer and Rugby were his main interests, though he knew more about Troilus and Criseyde than anyone thought he needed to. Bits have been falling off him for years, but luckily he met Sandra before too much had. A man who cheers you up just by thinking about him.

But singing or not, these were the last days of the Commune.

My three communards brought women round on approval.

Alan embraced Jenny among the collapsing fruit box bookshelves in his rosy-cheeked box room. Dave looked enough like a Beatle for Marilyn to come over from America on a single ticket to ride. And I heard Malcolm and Sandra laughing in bed before it was even dark, and I'd never heard that before.

*

We had a few last months at Belmont Hill in Lewisham in a big house with greenhouses and wives-to-be and a cat called Arthur.

We had parties there too, but with dips.

Another George who played another guitar joined us, and it was this second George who got the bollocking when the owners came back and found just him with the bust hoover trying to clear up, on the day the Commune died.

They all got married. I came home.

But long after, on long walks and long unsleepy nights, I've told my children Eleanor and Megan and Goronwy some of the heroic tales from the days of the Commune, to encourage them not to get bourgeoisified[93] too soon.

I probably lied a bit, like you do.[94]

---

93 My Megan writes, from her new home down south, 'I think I might be bourgeoisified now. I'm just heading out to buy a baking tray.'

94 My Eleanor was working in London this year and txtd me - 'just stopped in maze hill and thought of u & the alan show & curries on friday & the yellow walls and mrs weaver. they are almost memories for me now - as though I had been there - how strange xx.' I feel the same about loads of my Mum and Dad's past lives too, especially now they've all been churned up again. For charity, though, remember?

Hirondelle, Golden Notebooks, Ginsberg[95]

1967 was the year Alan Ginsberg levitated the Pentagon to stop the Vietnam War. It was also the year of *Bob Dylan's Greatest Hits* on the first stereo hi fi.

It found me living in a filthy room in downtown Greenwich.

Greenwich England, that is.

I was an English teacher in a 2500-pupil London comprehensive school. The kids were great by 67. They came round at weekends to the sort of teachers' commune we had in this little semi by the park.

We wrote experimental novels and free verse and made surreal films. We did strange plays, went to the theatre, walked and talked.

Sgt Pepper was everywhere turning everything suddenly into colour, even the telly.

Things were getting kinder. Homosexuality was legal. The new abortion act was passing. There was a Labour government and that one wasn't joining any Americans on a war for democracy half way across the world.

And there's one more thing in my summer of 67.

Only two of us know this, and she will have forgotten, if she even noticed at the time.

But suddenly in 1967, if you signed a form at the birth control clinic in New Cross that your girl was your fiancée, she could get the Pill.

At the third attempt I did, and she did. And, not before time, we did.

The Summer of Love indeed.

She was a painter in an attic off Blackheath. It was a dusty sunny Saturday afternoon that smelt of linseed.

It was touch and go.

---

95 Written (without fee) for a forty-years-on Summer of Love feature in the Telegraph.

A Whiter Shade of Pale was playing. We had just been reading *The Golden Notebook*.

We drank Hirondelle after, like grown ups.

Heroics
or
Boy George And Me On A Sofa Down The Wicker

John Cleese in the film *Clockwise* is a London comprehensive school headmaster who watches his pupils from his office through binoculars, so that he can tell them off over his tannoy.

Peter Dawson who arrived at Eltham Green School in the summer term of 1970 used binoculars like that, and was the inspiration for Cleese's headmaster.

Eight weeks after he did arrive, on the very last day I could, without talking to anybody, I resigned in a one-sentence letter.

It's the only time I've ever behaved unambiguously honourably, irritatingly, unarguably morally, on a matter of high principle, whatever the cost to me.

I'd been at Eltham Green for seven years.

I was Deputy Head of English by then and, with James Learmonth[96] and Geoff Hacker, was producing our *Conflict* English source books that sold hundreds of thousands, and were for a bit the texts of what was sometimes called the *New English.*[97]

It was not English as we knew it, and Eltham Green wasn't the only school getting rid of Ridout the textbook, clause analysis, ten-question comprehensions, essays, handwriting, elocution, middle class white men's novels and dead white men poets' poems. Instead we'd have working class literature, black literature, women's literature, writeyourownpoems literature, experimental course work novels, talking, acting, screen, media and role-play.

And fun.

I was as happy as I've ever been, teaching this New English at Eltham Green. I would have stayed for ever with Pauline, Deborah, Janice, David, Christine, the Other Janice, Janet, Harriet, Valerie, Clive, John, Maureen,

---

96 A man who could imitate an owl with his tongue, and the finest educationalist of my time. He and his Maggie should have had more time themselves.
97 Nelson published them and about another 30 English source books and plays and novels I did. We sold the first two Conflict books for £90 each. They would have made us very rich. The other books didn't, and I never was. NEVER SIGN AWAY YOUR ROYALTIES!

Leslie, Lesley, Colin, Susan, Denis, Barbara, Lizzie, Billy, Bill, Noel, Brian, Satinder, Tony –

Not that Eltham Green itself was exactly Summerhill, yet.

But there was art hanging all over the building, and we had our own theatre for making shows and films. The staff weren't all beautiful people with flowers in their hair, but some of us were, and we were getting younger and hairier by the term. There were nearly more of us than them.

Yes, there were still gowns. And streaming. And setting. And reports. And detentions. There were still prefects, and uniforms. And shouting. All round us there were still selective schools and religious and fee-paying schools so we were never a comprehensive comprehensive anyway. On Speech Days the Head's best proof that we worked was one pupil from the poshest bit of Blackheath who once got to Oxford.

There was still a pastoral system[98] the old Head had created with eight Houses named -

> **E**ndeavour
> **L**oyalty
> **T**ruthfulness
> **H**onesty
> **A**mbition
> **M**odesty
> **G**enerosity
> **S**incerity.[99]

But the new Labour Government was on our side. And history.

We knew that as soon as someone younger came in to co-run with us the biggest comprehensive in England, with a bit of energy, a love of kids, a sense of fun, and the enthusiasm to unstream and democratise, de-school and re-school and –

                                        *

---

98 For the sheep. That was something else that would have to go.

99 The first letter of each line read out vertically spells out the name of the school. At football inter-house competitions the kids with glasses on the touchlines had to shout, 'Come on Sincerity!' And, 'Put some effort in, Truthfulness!' And, 'Kick them where it hurts Generosity!' I was in Ambition house. My commune housemate Dave Wasp was in Modesty. When he got promotion he became Head of Ambition.

And what we got was Dawson.

Before his first term started, he'd ordered all the kids' art to be removed.

He put his *New English Bible* and a book about *Nixon* and *Leadership* on the empty bookshelves in his office.

He shouted at kids in public for being where they shouldn't, and at the staff, and in public, for not being where they should.

He did everything at a shout, and boasted in shouting assemblies and loud meetings about all the people he'd recently caught out and punished.

He was too bothered about how we all dressed, though he was a dim dresser himself, in dark suits too big on such a little man, in his heavy glasses and brylcreem.

He suddenly materialised in corridors and corners.

He smirked.

He showed off in assemblies, using Methodist visual aids.

He censored school shows.

He opposed trade unions.

And sex.

And children's rights

And he spied with binoculars and ended up in *Clockwise.*

*

He wrote a book about it, after, teaching everyone the secret of taming a school. He called it *The Road From Bomb Alley.*[100]

His secret weapon on that Road wasn't shouting, materialising, smirking, showing off, censoring, or spying.

---

100 He wrote, 'If ever there was an occupation in which it pays not to take oneself too seriously teaching is it…a teacher must have a sense of humour.' He must have been joking.

And it wasn't secret either, and it changed everything.

It was the cane.[101]

*

Now caning was still legal in 1970, but what little of it that was going on at Eltham Green was done in secret by a couple of the highest-paid teachers on the same few damaged boys.

Not on girls of course. And that's another argument we should have taken to the big staff, parent and kid consultation meetings about the proposed changes to policy on corporal punishment in our school.

And we should also have asked what kind of relationships there can ever be between young and old, teacher and taught, when the old hit the young for not agreeing. Or threaten to. And need to deter every boy in the school with a deterrent that doesn't work because, if it did, you'd never need to use it, certainly not repeatedly on the same damaged kids. And we should also have asked why, if it's OK to hit them, it isn't it OK for them to hit each other? And when they're bigger, us?[102] And what might be the effect on them when they become parents? Citizens? And what did it teach the kids who didn't get caned? Or the girls?

Big questions for the big consultation meetings.

*

But there weren't any consultation meetings.

There was just a new headmaster chosen for us by people we'd never met.

He said there was going to be more caning. Done by more staff. On more boys. Kids and parents couldn't do anything about it. If some teachers were too poorly-paid to be allowed, or had other problems with it, then they could report boys to someone higher up who would do their caning for them.

Not could. Had to.

---

101 Up till him, in this school of two and a half thousand kids with five gyms and a library on its roof, and its own theatre, you could mostly get lost if you wanted, and do what you wanted if the kids didn't mind and you filled in the registers.

102 I shook little 12-year-old Raymond (2B5) in room 314 till he cried, after school one night in my second year teaching. He didn't mind, after. I never hit a kid again.

(Unambiguously honourably, irritatingly, unarguably morally, matter of high principle moment whatever the cost to me, coming up.)

*

At first I thought I could just ignore it.

Occupy some oppositional space.

Have classroom discussions and debates about corporal punishment.

Still read James Joyce' pandybat schooldays with classes.

The kids could know where I stood on a principle and how interesting principles are. And what oppositional space is, and how say Brecht dealt with the Un-American Activities lot, and what the Diggers did. And Martin Luther King and Blair Peach.

My pupils could make up their own minds, and negotiate their own ways round what they didn't believe to be right. They could refuse to be caned. Volunteer to be caned. Tell their Dads to come up. The posher kids from Blackheath who'd never get caned but who hated what the cane was doing to their school could organise and occupy. Burgle, and snap all the canes. Passively resist by all putting their hands out together. Cane each other in public.

And the NUT could get organised and we could write an article for the *Times Educational Supplement* and join *S.T.O.P.P.* And –

*

The trouble was that my room, 314, was exactly opposite a boy's lavatory. It had never been pleasant in there, so for years I'd locked it up before morning break, for the rest of the day, with a key stolen from the caretaker.

Dawson decided to crack down on smoking. Under the new regime, all lavatories had to stay unlocked all day, so boys who wanted to go in there to smoke were free to do so, so they could then be caught, so that they could then be caned, so that everyone could then be told, so they wouldn't do it again, so when they did do it again they could be caught and caned and everyone could be told again. And again.

Not could be caught. Had to be. And had to be publicly exposed in assembly, as well, before being privately caned.

I puzzled for a bit to see how I could get round that.

Could I police the lav myself? Ask the kids not to smoke, as a favour to me? But wouldn't word get round the 2500 kids that there was this one lav opposite 314 where you could smoke and not get caned, you'd just get old Robbo being all disappointed and pretending he couldn't smell your smoke?

I'd have to lurk round that lav all day silently begging kids I didn't know not to put me in an impossible position. When I should be in Room 314 enjoying imagination, fun, creativity, love?

Until by mistake I'd find some kid unarguably at it.

If I didn't report him then? Or couldn't? Or did?

I resigned in that one-sentence letter.

*

I'm the only teacher named in Dawson's book and he quotes me several times. He didn't show such respect when I privately then publicly explained my problem with his caning. I believe he did his best to make sure I never worked again.

In his book (without asking) he also uses a real poem written in room 314 one last lesson on an uncaned afternoon by my pupil Christine French.

*

Years later I saw him smirking towards me on a train just outside Derby. I made sure I didn't recognise him.

Some years after that, I was sitting on a sofa with Boy George doing an outside broadcast from a recording studio on the Wicker in Sheffield. He'd also expelled himself from Eltham Green in early Dawson days.

I told him, off air, about my principled decision, my Thomas More moment. And my brave speech in the Hall in front of the staff, governors, press, and the kids serving the drinks, on my last day, after we had stripped room 314 of all the kids' poems and paintings and slogans and photos. And after all the last presents had been exchanged, and all the (kept) promises made that we'd be pals for ever. And the carefully sober moment when I stepped forward and from my script said -

I don't suppose I should say this, and here go my references for another job in teaching, but I have to say this, because I want to tell you why I am leaving this school and what the matter of principle is. I -

Boy George had never heard of my principled resignation.

He didn't remember me.

I think he giggled and said he'd rather have had a cup of tea.

*

I was out of work for a year, and never got any job I applied for, even when I was the only interviewee. But then got made Head of English at J K Turner's[103] Sedgehill School on the Friday I read on the train to Beckenham Junction that my just-published novel[104] was -

> *Very funny*
> New Statesman

I had tea after the interview with two of the teachers who would now be under me in my staff of fifteen women (things looking up generally by now), both of whom I would in time love and be loved by.

My own Road from Bomb Alley wasn't turning out to be quite as stony as it could have been.[105]

*

My novel finishes with Christine French's (paid-for) poem.

If I Were The Sun

If I were the sun
And I saw the things that people have done
I would eclipse myself
For ever.

---

103 The only headmaster I've ever respected. He wasn't afraid of the kids, or of looking a fool, and he couldn't be bothered to read other people's references. Or presumably their books.

104 The Ted Carp Tradition (Hodder) about life in a huge comprehensive school, finished and with my agent (Pat Kavanagh!) five months before Dawson. It was accepted three weeks after I resigned, by the sixth publisher it had been sent to. I lived off the £300 advance, and my parents back in Sheffield, till I finally get a job again. The publisher chose the title. I wanted to call it 'Class!'

105 My daughter Megan says I once said this was one of the happiest days of my life.

J Is For Genius
or
The Man Who Cremated Himself

Instead of essays, when I was an experimental English teacher, pupils wrote poems and films and stories and ballads and Beatle songs - and experimental novels.

This kid, after two terms of homework, handed in a Swan matchbox full of burned paper. A note explained that it was all that was left of the long autobiography of an experimental novelist who had written his life in loose sheets as he remembered it, but who had then decided that he had not been experimental enough. So he'd cremated himself.

Jessop Returns

My Dear John,

I feel I must write and express my congratulations to you on the success of your creation. I know how wonderful I felt nearly 30 years ago when I produced 3¾ pounds of manhood! Even then Nanny Jessop predicted a great future for you! I thought perhaps she was trying to console me for such a minute effort, but as you know jewels are only produced in small quantities, although some might reply so is poison - yet we can choose the one we prefer. I shall certainly push the book once it's out and I've already prepared Geth Snr. about its possible bawdiness.

Love, Lily

J Is Also For Jammy
or
Radio Sheffield Changed My Life

Dave Sheasby,[106] then Education Producer at Radio Sheffield, recorded me in the Ballroom at 60 Westbourne Road talking about the just-published *Ted Carp Tradition*, for the breakfast programme the following morning.

The Ballroom was this vast space on the first floor, which was later turned into studios.

Anyway, the following morning Ed Thomason, who'd just started directing *Theatre Vanguard* from the (not yet open) Crucible was in Broomhill with a VHF radio and a new girl friend, and was up early enough to hear the breakfast interview.[107]

He rang to ask me to write him a play.

I became a playwright for the rest of my life.

---

106 D J H Sheasby. King Edward's, the LSE and then Sheffield for ever. Saturnine playwright, poet, tipster, wit, educationalist, director, garden sculptor, runner, garden centre apparatchik, radio man, father of six. Known since teenage days by some of us as Fritz. In our final e-mails we couldn't remember why.
107 I never met anybody else who did, even me, because I wasn't up for breakfast and we hadn't got VHF in Totley anyway.

Just Sit Up Straight And Try To Be Grown Up About It

No sooner had I become a playwright than I became a sex education teacher as well.

I'd published that novel, been asked to be a playwright, then done a couple of months on supply at Woodthorpe School in Sheffield being useless

That had been followed by a useless month in Brittany with an old friend who'd become a new lover and then wished she hadn't. She was also one of my staff of fifteen women at my new school. As we struggled in the August mists down by Cap Frehel, drinking chocolat chaud and still hoping for the best, she said how she thought they must put something in the school dinners at her/my school because, she said, the entire staff was always at It.

I supposed at the time that she was telling me to make up for our August uselessnesses, but when I got there in September I found she was right, only more so.

Half the staff was under thirty, many just coming up to the end of their first marriages. The most unlikely people were unpairing, repairing and pairing again. Before parents' evenings. And after. At jumble sales, on theatre visits, sports days, and PTA spelling bees. In changing rooms, cloakrooms, dining rooms, stock rooms, staff rooms, medical rooms, visual aids rooms, cupboards, gyms, and corridors. At lunchtime, teatime, playtime, before school, after detentions, and at any old times at all.

I had - have - never had a love-life like it.

*

Anyway, someone must have been talking, because at the start of my second year I was summonsed by the Head and told that all Third Years would now do one lesson a week of Personal Relationships Including Sex led by the Deputy Head, the Head of Third Year - and the Head of English. There was no budget and no syllabus but there was a big room that was only ever used for exams, with an overhead projector and curtains.

He'd leave the details to us.

Now, the Deputy Head was unmarried, to put it mildly, and more into dogs.

The Head of Third Year was a single mother who'd not shown much interest in sex, so far, which was unusual at Sedgehill.

And the Head of English was me, fizzing with It, having, to be honest, never previously having gone All The Way in his own personal relationships till the age of 26.[108]

*

So, anyway once a week, Personal Relationships Including Sex.

We started with Smoking, using filmstrips and ourselves, exhaling into handkerchiefs and showing the Third Year how yellow our breath was.

Then we did Bullying, Telling Stories and Drinking.

Then it was Christmas, so we did Christmas.

In the first part of the spring term the room was needed for mock exams, so we did multiple-choice revision of Smoking, Bullying, Telling Stories, Drinking, and Christmas, in small rooms.

Mock exams over, we had Dog Breeds, the Importance of Being Married and then - when we hold back no longer - we had Sex.

*

Sex?

My Mum had never told us anything, except to wash our charlies properly with a flannel.

My Dad's only advice to us was not to take girls out for meals, or sleep when there were sailors about.

The Seniors at All Saints had told us in J3 what you had to do, but who'd want to?

I'd read Dad's *News of the World* for years of course, like everyone did in case they were in it. So I knew that sometimes intimacy did take place, but when it did you'd end up in court, sure as a scoutmaster.

---

108 So? Bernard Shaw was 29.

At King Edward's we had been careful not to sit next to the High School girls on the Number 9 Circular in case we caught VD. We mainly used whatever came to hand, though there were two pages in *Green's Biology* we knew off by heart, about vestibules and fallopian tubes.

At Oxford I had to be celibate because of my Keble scholarship but there were 17 men to every posh woman anyway.

Once I got to London some intimacies did take place, until at last, one linseed afternoon in Blackheath -

> *We skipped the light fandango*
> *As the miller told his tale*

And here I was only five years later, teaching Sex to the entire Third Year.

*

The Deputy Head decreed that the best way was to call It Reproduction and deal with Questions as and when, and try to be grown up about It.

> *Just sit up and try to be grown up! There is nothing to laugh at is*
> *there Mr Robinson?*

First she led a couple of inaccurate sessions using slides of the private parts of Damien Hurst. And then -

> *Write your anonymous question down. Only one each thank you.*
> *Don't talk about it! Best writing, for if we can't read your handwriting*
> *I'm sorry it will have to go straight in the bin. Ditto if anyone's silly*
> *enough to be try to be silly. Don't be embarrassed. We have seen it*
> *all before haven't we Mr Robinson?*

We got plenty of anonymous questions.

> *Are you sure It can't make you blind?*
> *What if you miss, Miss?*
> *How long should It last?*
> *Can other people tell if you have done It, after?*
> *How can you be sure you have?*
> *This is a scale drawing of my friend's private parts, should they be*
> *like this, Miss?*
> *What's the difference between going all the way and getting off the*

98

54 at the pub at the corner to Beckenham where some of the buses
turn round anyway?
How old were you when you first went all the way Mr Robinson?
Do Dalmatians's spots rub off during coition?
Please Miss where's my clematis, only it wasn't on the diagram?
Can you burst yourself?
What do you have to do?[109]

We couldn't read most of the handwriting, so we had to put most of the questions straight in the bin. And make up our own.[110]

*

The following year the Headmaster decreed that the Third Years should do Citizenship, starting with Handwriting, then Smoking, Drinking, Christmas, How to Revise, The Separation of Powers In The British Constitution, the -

But by then I'd run away to join the theatre.

---

109 A few year ago the BBC reporter Steph Hyner was out in the streets asking Radio Sheffield men about what they knew about sex and this bloke told her to switch off the light, love, and hope for the best.

110 My own kids' Sex Education teacher, nine years ago, had to have the Headmaster sitting at the back of her class while she blushed her way through her own Damien Hurst diagrams on the PowerPoint, and the usual handwritten questions. When they were doing the importance of contraception, a girl produced a condom. She got reported to the Governors. And her father.

6. What I Told The Policeman

Keep Moving

Wait for the Bell by the *Crucible Theatre Vanguard* (the first show I got paid for) was performed in *Lucky's Drama Studio*, formerly the carpet warehouse under the Old Chapel on Scotland Street, and at the *Oval House* in London, where it got me into trouble.

The show was a sort of revue about education then, now, and soon. The audience sat at school desks, and were regularly told off and tested by the actors. There were sketches, playlets and readings from the *Little Red Schoolbook*, with songs and poems.

> *Unwieldy, brave experiment…its pretensions are greater than its performance and ultimately it falls between two stools.*
> Paul Allen (Morning Telegraph)

It was fun for us, though, so we did some more.

*

Edward Carpenter Lives! was the second-ever play in the *Sheffield Crucible Studio* and the first to transfer to the Main House.

It was also my first proper play -

> *Set in Sheffield after the revolution, a new play by Rony Robinson, directed by Ed Thomason. 40p Students and OAPs 25p*

It tells of one Friday in the life of Town Hall wallah and matrimonially-challenged Harold Beck, an enthusiastic secret follower of the Victorian radical Edward Carpenter.[111] Beck's job in the Water Department, registering taps and hosepipes in ledgers, is driving him mad. As is his tennis club wife. And to add to all that, on this particular May Friday, his *New Statesman* hasn't arrived.

At the same time some actors are rehearsing scenes from a play on the life of Edward Carpenter, at the *Crucible*.[112]

---

111 You find them all over the place. We hope that John the Swan, who is one, will write the definitive memoir of us.

112 They are presumably the Crucible Theatre Vanguard Company who are actually doing my actual play.

I truanted from my London school and crept into the *Crucible Studio* just in time for the last ten minutes of the Dress Rehearsal to find Harold Beck had just come home.

This is *The Song of Harold Beck* -

> *There's a family of thieves own some steelworks*
> *And a house out on Hathersage Moor*
> *They've an aunt lives in Bents Green*
> *Who's big on the rents scene*
> *They'll just not exist any more.*
> *From Fulwood's fanciest flatlets*
> *To Tinsley's teemingest slums*
> *Come rain or shine*
> *And not before time*
> *The Revolution comes!*

All the people I'd made up in my bedroom were all there, on Red Friday, and were all jumping into the baths at Glossop Road –

> *All the swimmers and the spectators, men women and children were stark bollock-naked and unconcerned with it!*

> *There were pinks and whites and blacks and bronzes, and two Chinese men I think I recognised from that restaurant near the Town Hall where I had chow mein on Fridays. I tugged -*

There were two hours to the opening of my show that was coming, ready or not, to my theatre, in my town.

I had come home too.

> *I tugged at my sweating clothing and ripped it off me in an ecstatic moment of freedom, leaping in at the deep end in the narrow space between an elderly man and a small West Indian lady who were clapping hands patacake style to the sound of the singing….*
> *Edward Carpenter Lives!*

*

A play that is too long, pretentious and very predictable so that even a very stylised production cannot redeem the static long literary passages…
The Star review of the opening night in the Studio.

If you're waiting for the Crucible to put on the right play, this is it. Simply the best production seen so far at the Crucible. A play for which Sheffield can be proud.
The Star review of the opening night in the Main House.

*

The real Edward Carpenter (1844-1929) came to Sheffield from Brighton and was an Anglican curate and mathematician who became an anarchist, vegetarian nudist, mystic sandal-making poetic anti-vivisectionist, clothes-reforming gay teetotalling socialist.

He lived round here half his life, including at Totley, and then at Millthorpe in the Cordwell valley just up from the *Royal Oak* in a back-to-front house he cobbled together for his sandal-making and market garden.

Sheila Rowbotham wrote the big book about him in 2008.

I've had several goes at him too.

The school is named after him in *The Ted Carp Tradition,* and the revolutionary schoolkids read from his books in the school library during their sit-in. He also gets taken on my *Beano* to Scarborough in 1914. He was in my first two Crucible plays and a later one at Coventry Belgrade.

I've dressed up as him at a party run for the *Edward Carpenter Community* at Unstone Grange, though nobody noticed on an extraordinary night that included the vivid re-enactment of the last time he had sex, a few days before he died at 85.

I've spent long ages with the Carpenter papers in Local Studies and Archives, and tried on his sandals and Saxon tunic.

With my Eleanor, when she was a student at Sussex, I've rung the bell on the door of his massive childhood home in Brighton, then run away.

I've stamped on his grave in Guildford,[113] and slept in his bed, or someone else's, in Millthorpe.

I've lectured on him at Oxford University, helped deliver a paper on his famous socialist marching song, all fifteen verses of it, at a top university international festival of working class music -

> *England arise! the long long night is over*
> > *Faint in the east behold the dawn appear*
> *Out of your evil dream of toil and sorrow-*
> > *Arise! O England, for the day is here.*

AJP Taylor ends his *Oxford History of the 20th Century* with the Labour victory of 1945, and a note about that hymn of Carpenter's -

> *The British Empire declined; the condition of the people improved. Few now sang Land of Hope and Glory. Few even sang England Arise. England had risen all the same.*

I've done telly and radio programmes about him. I'm on YouTube with him, just. I've got a signed picture of him in his sandals above my desk now as I write this.

My mother met him as a girl when she was taken out with the Sheffield Independent Labour Party in a wagonnette.

Nanny Chandler told me he was -

> *Rum. He grew potatoes out of season and lived with a manservant like she was his wife.*

---

113 Twenty years ago there was a gig at his grave in Guildford.
Sheila Rowbotham was there and so was the Red Vicar of Darnall. And various beardies, a man who looked a bit risky, and me, as fraternal delegate from Sheffield Trades and Labour. The grave is as undistinguished as Guildford, except for two things. Lewis Carroll is just over the wall. And it's a joint grave with Carpenter's dead gay lover George Merrill. We nearly sang England Arise but didn't quite dare. It's too easily mixed up with Christians Awake, and it also has a very high note at the end. I hope he didn't hear us not singing. But last year there was an Edward Carpenter Walk, and by a stile, in a Millthorpe field, Sheila, Sally Goldsmith and I led the crackly singing, and Edward Carpenter lived on.

King Lear, Joseph of Arimathea and Ma Brown

Meanwhile in Coventry, there were *Events in an Upper Room,* using my script from actors' workshops, telling what happened after Jesus left the Last Supper, only this time He was in modern dress in Northern Ireland.

It closed quietly without the London critics exactly rushing.

But the morning after it did, Harold Hobson of *The Sunday Times* published a huge review under the title *Shared Vision*. He said how wonderful the actors were, especially Michael Gough as Joseph of Arimathea.

And went on to say -

> *The play ought to be seen in London at the Royal Court if the Royal Court did not seem traditionally disinclined not to put on this kind of play.*
> Sunday Times.

The *Royal Court* was on the phone first thing Monday, asking for it, and the play did get seen in London, though in the end at the *ICA.*

I tampered with it, the actors were shakier on the lines, and it never worked again, either in London or wherever else it was revived.

Harold Hobson himself was from South Yorkshire, took a History degree at Oxford, and is of course the greatest theatre critic there ever was.

Though a shocking writer.

> *If the Royal Court did not seem traditionally disinclined not to put on this kind of play.*

Eh?

*

Coventry was also where I rewrote my *A Time of Bears* as a novel from a play I wrote for the Crucible from a play I wrote for Sedgehill School with a real bear and the mysterious and fragmentary Valerie Jane Challenger as Martha.

The King and his court are at the Cold Season palace. Towards them a group of travelling players are making their way slowly through the frozen land. In a distant village a young woman gives shelter to a stranger she finds sleeping in the road. Out of these mysterious fragments Rony Robinson builds up, in A Time of Bears, a novel that is almost mythical in its bleak and compelling beauty.
Selena Hastings (Daily Telegraph)

Compelling beauty, *moi!*

It's the fifth of my books for kids that have girl heroes, only this time she is a girl pretending to be a boy playing the girls' parts in a company of travelling players, till she turns out to be Cordelia, King Lear's runaway daughter.

Towards the end of her story, she makes a speech about why theatre so matters -

> **CORDELIA**
> We can't be happy pretending to be like other people.
> We aren't like other people.
> The ordinary thing for us is to be extraordinary.
> We're everybody.
> We make crowds silent and we become animals and jugglers and women and - we can't just stop?

The players are persuaded to do one more show, and it leads them all to the nearest thing to a happy ending there is (or was, then).

*

Macmillan bought the book just as I was running away to really join the travelling players myself.

I'd done a second year at the *Belgrade Theatre* in Coventry, got a bike, and some mucky digs up near the old football ground. I'd stuck up some posters, drunk some beer at *Ma Browns* and the *Town Wall,* fallen among actors and sort of forgotten to go back teaching.

Oh and got into trouble again.

*

King Better

Friday 27th September 1974

You presented a Coventry platform ticket number 10366 to the Ticket Collector on duty at the ticket barrier at Coventry Railway Station.

You went to number 3b platform and sat on a bench reading a newspaper. You were kept under observation by a Police Officer. At 7.06 the 7.03 pm train to Birmingham arrived and you boarded it.

The Police Officer made himself known to you and told you he had reason to believe you were in possession of a platform ticket.

You told the officer you were in possession of a platform ticket and that you would pay the fare when you arrived at Sheffield, as you didn't have time to buy a valid ticket.

You said, 'If I leave this train I will miss my connection to Sheffield.'
You left the train and began to accompany the Officer to the ticket barrier.

As you were walking across the footbridge you said to the Officer, 'It is a pity that you have nothing fucking better to do than fuck about like this.'

At the ticket barrier the Officer told you that he had observed you on the platform for about five minutes and you could have bought a valid ticket during this period.

You replied, 'I arrived at the station at seven o' clock. There being a small queue at the ticket office I put a two-penny piece in the platform ticket machine and purchased a platform ticket. I ran to platform three where I fully expected the 1903 train to Birmingham to be. I sat down on a bench and began to read today's New Statesman paper.

When the train arrived I boarded it. A man who was a Policeman suggested I got off the train thus missing my connection to Sheffield. In some anger at the implication that I was travelling fraudulently and suggesting to this policeman that he might have better things to do I accompanied him to the ticket barrier and made this statement, using some bad language en route.'

The Officer told you that the facts would be reported and that you may be prosecuted and cautioned.
You replied 'No.'[114]

---

114 I pleaded not guilty. I wouldn't take the oath. I had no lawyer. My defence from the dock was as follows - if you'd charged me with using some bad language en route, like you were originally going to, I would have pleaded guilty. But I am not guilty on this charge because you have to prove my intention was to avoid paying. Only I know my intention. My intention was not to avoid paying. I won the case, shook hands with the police officer and came home. By train. I had been before the beak once before after a Committee of a 100 anti-nuclear sit-down passive disobedience protest. I began a heroic speech from the dock then too, but the Magistrate said he wasn't interested in the survival of the planet, only in the free flow of traffic on Marylebone High Street, and he fined me forty shillings with thirty shillings costs. Which my Dad paid. Oh, and I hadn't fiddled the railways. My Mum always told me what a totally honest man her beloved Dad, my Grandy, was, and why he had to be, if he was a socialist.

Kerchiefs, Smocks and Satchels

By the time the proofs of *A Time of Bears* arrived I was in midwinter Burnley doing a play about a 1960's mining disaster, living in digs with two actors (1m, 1f), a bust cooker, no heating and two beds between the three of us.

> *With his Santa Claus smile, and the compassionate eyes of a father confessor, his satchel, smock and red kerchief, Rony Robinson looks like an advertising agency's idea of an itinerant poet.*
> Robin Thornber[115] (Guardian)

With satchel, smock and kerchief, I itineranted all over.

I got the cheapest digs, and lived a few months at a time like the actors, on actors' wages, going to all the rehearsals and performances, and having all the fun after, and creating like mad.

And was myself re-created.

In Cheshire I worked with giggling, clever Chris Honer, who was also a bit of a Santa-smiling compassionate man himself. We made up daring shows from people's stories, one-night standing all over the north with a van and no props, costume, lights or curtains. Chris's stage version of *The Beano* at Derby was terrific and we only just missed cracking something really new with Paul McCleary's[116] Buttons in a *Cinderella*.

Still itineranting, I co-wrote the dodgy first stage versions of *The Hobbit* and they played huge theatres, made loads of money, went in and out of the West End twice, and then bankrupted everybody. Graham Watkins and I made a better job of Roald Dahl's *Matilda*, and that went into town too, and I had a ham salad at Dahl's pad and poked in his writing shed.

I worked with Bob Carlton with his raincoat, moustache and cigarettes, in Lancashire villages doing prototypes of *Return To The Forbidden Planet*. We had Shakespeare and the whole cast doing the music, magic, escapology and anything else that filled the stage, with so many things going on at the

---

115 Robin Thornber drove me home from a first night in Leicester and twice ran out of petrol. Luckily he belonged to both the RAC and the AA. The last time we spoke was in 2010 on the radio - I'd been set a Sunday challenge to find a Robin or a Hood because of a new film. I said on air I wish he'd ring because he was a great critic, and the only Robin I knew. But he was already ringing, from Glossop, because his daughter Lucy had tipped him off. She said, after, that he was famous at last.
116 Paul read the staff-breaking from The Tempest at the woodland burial of our pal Peter Cheeseman, kneeling in the bluebells at the open grave and daring to do it more slowly than I've ever heard. It was Shakespearian.

same time that nobody noticed not much was. Our anti-royal *Duke's Jubilee* included the most shocking moment I've managed in the theatre so far, when at the end of the Carnforth first night (and only then) we played the National Anthem, and half the audience stood while the other half laughed at them. Bob and I later rehearsed a play for a pier at Morecambe that got a rave review in the Stage, even though it was never performed in front of any audience.

I did two shows for DAC, the heroic Doncaster shoebox, butterscotch seat-of-everyone's-pants-carnival-Grotowski-poor-with-added-beer theatre. Skiddy as a November Handicap. And as Ron Rose himself, the Donnygate whistle-blower, who founded it and scrounged for it, lured the talent to it, and proved that running your own theatre was as easy as falling off a roof.

I had a lot of fun with Jonathan Chadwick too, my curly communist friend taking Brecht-ish shows to annoy old people in East London and then turning them into Snapshots for The Theatre Royal Stratford East.[117]

Snapshots is the only show I've ever done that everybody liked.

> *Exuberant fleet footed and altogether likeable.*
> John Barber (Daily Telegraph)

It's the story of an East End girl growing up between the wars. Deborah Findlay was wonderful in it, especially in the best scene I ever wrote, about a man trying to sell a second-hand suit to her on the streets of London in 1936. He tells his tale of that suit, how he bought it on credit so he could pawn it so he could get food for his wife. But with the loan repayments, he soon got back into debt, and had to buy another more expensive suit also to pawn, to pay his debt on the first one and still feed his wife. Deborah says she is sorry she can't afford to buy the suit from him, though she can understand why his wife is crying. The man says his wife is not crying about the suits, she is crying because King Edward has just abdicated.

I wrote it overnight in the last week of rehearsals, and took it to Jonathan in the morning. It went straight into the show just as it was, and got applause wherever it went, including in Amsterdam in thick snow.

---

117 Home of Joan Littlewood's O What a Lovely War and now me. Joan Littlewood herself had turned up to address the Sixth Form at Sedgehill School and spent her whole talk sending the audience in and out, eventually making us come in pretending to be the person next to us. She never took off her hat and I think she was drunk. I hope so.

Snapshots also used *verbatim* accounts of 1930s East London lives we'd collected. Including this conversation[118] –

THERESA
They were the good old days weren't they? The only way to get a little bit of extra money was, if you want a bit of crumpet you pay for it. Well it's the only way you got it. It's right innit? You had about fourpence in your purse to go and you said, *All right mate give us a tanner.* No, it's right innit? You had four pence to get over the next day and the old man come home pissed, if he wanted a bit of crumpet, 4d. There's your dinner.

MERVYN
It's the cream of the East End aint it?

BOB
Salt of the earth.

MERVYN
Old Arthur'd be flattered if he heard you wouldn't he?

THERESA
We used to sleep in separate rooms. So there's some knocking on the walls and he's shouting, *You'll be surprised what I'm knocking this wall with.* No, he aint got nothing there now. Have you seen it? No, I don't like looking at it now. I feel sorry when I see it now cos there's nothing there now. I feel sorry for it now cos there's nothing there. It's like a little boy's. It's a shame innit when they go little like that. When you think years ago it was big as this stick. Used to make my head bang. That's right innit?

BOB
As big as that stick?

MERVYN
If your Arthur had one as big as that they ought to put him in the bleeding museum.

THERESA
I mean if you can't get across the river you could walk over the bridge over it. Couldn't you Jack? You put yours on the table and show us. And you put yours in Omo Fred, don't half make it come up bright.

MERVYN
As big as that stick? Ought to be in a bleeding museum.

BOB
Tell him you told us he'd got one big as that, and I'll ask him to show us.

---

118 Much later, Sally Goldsmith made a Yorkshire song version of this conversation in Last Loves, our Sony award winning radio play. It was wonderfully sung by the wonderful Monica Mellor from Firth Park.

THERESA
No he will show you if you ask him. Cos I'm frightened to look at it now.

*

I worked with Rob Swain and others for Peter Cheeseman my, everyone's hero[119] in both *Vics* in Stoke, doing documentaries about potters, joggers, Haydns, Stanley Matthewses, and plays with string quartets and autoharps.

I worked with the film director Danny Hiller on a tiny country music play *Goodbye America*, and he made it, and us, and Suffolk sing. We're lifelong collaborators because of it, and one day we're going to do something brilliant.

I worked everywhere with Gary Yershon, the most talented music man in English theatre, and we've shared digs a few times too, but say no more. Our greatest hit is a chirpy long-ago song about a coach operator in Chester in 1935. I'd hoped Gary would be at the launch of these memoirs so that in a *coup de theatre*, as I read out this paragraph, he would stumble from the back, like the volunteer organist himself -

> *The scene was one I'll ne'er forget*
> *As long as I may live*
> *And just to see it one more time*
> *All earthly joys I'd give*

and give us Henry Farrell one more time.

*

For ten years I lived the actor's life, always with a next opening night to look forward to.

I wrote over a hundred plays, one-at-a-time, in Lancaster, Dalston, Rotherham, Leeds, Birmingham, Farnham, Leicester, Stoke, Manchester, Morecambe (nearly), Hampstead, Lincolnshire, Doncaster - everywhere.

There were kids plays, community plays, adaptations, adopted plays, music plays, site specific plays, melodramatic plays, plays for socialists, plays for puppeteers, rewrites, new writes, pinches, operatic plays, therapeutic plays, megjepson plays, plays with free sweets, outdoor plays, plays with football in them (two), tiny plays, huge plays, very long plays, very short plays - and just play plays.

---

119 Though I'd say Romy Cheeseman was a bit of a hero too.

We're everybody. We make crowds silent and we become animals and jugglers and women and - we can't just stop.

The satchel, smock and kerchief days, eh?[120]

*

Still itinerant, I came back to the *Crucible* for *One Day in Sheffield,* which was a documentary about May 6th 1978.

All the words spoken in the play were real, but we allowed made-up punk songs and a narrator who'd obviously read his Dylan Thomas.

During rehearsals I got increasingly unsure about this *verbatim theatre* we were reinventing in the red footsteps of Ewan McColl,[121] Charles Parker, and Peter Cheeseman.

Would real people's real lives and the real ways they tell them make interesting theatre?

Would audiences come away with more respect for each other?

Be more hopeful?

Were there things that this sort of theatre could do that radio and telly and film - and plays - couldn't?

Can you have a new democratic theatre, this way? Stories about the people in their own words, performed in their own spaces?

*

On opening night I dangled up in the scaffolding outside the *Crucible Studio* lighting box, terrified of the height and of the coming disaster.

The dress rehearsal had seemed so small, after we'd collected so much. The actors seemed to be parodying the people. The whole show seemed to be

---

120 I wasn't the only one. We even had our own trade union - The Theatre Writers Union that agitated for a living wage for playwrights and met on Sunday afternoons in empty theatres. The usual suspects included John Arden, Caryl Churchill, David Edgar, Edward Bond, and Steve Gooch. I wrote more plays than any of them, was never as famous as any of them, and lived off it for years. Somebody should have done a play about us.

121 I met McColl at a scanty concert at Goldsmith's College. I asked him at the interval if he would do The Manchester Rambler and he said he wouldn't. Peggy Seeger was there too though, and she played Peggy Gordon in the second half, and that was the night I fell in lifelong love with the Appalachian Autoharp.

about to prove that it was only the educated and posh who had stories that deserved telling, and ways of speaking that deserved hearing.

But -

With an audience in, it worked. The company[122] could trust what we'd harvested and hardly needed to act at all.

That night was as wonderful as it gets.

We ran for three weeks, then the scripts and tapes were dumped in Local Studies at the Central Library, and the play vanished.

Like most plays do, and should.

(Who wants yesterday's papers?)

*

Among the hundreds of voices that spoke in our lost show of May 1978 is the Happy Lady, who started us off.

> **HAPPY LADY**
> I burned myself rather badly last night. I've just been along to the chemist to get some stuff and a nice young girl said, 'I'll do it for you', and she promptly bound it all up, and she did it very nicely. And what I wanted to say was, I've lived only the last four years in Sheffield. I only wanted to say I think Sheffield people don't know how lucky they are to live in Sheffield. It's the friendliest place I've known.

Then it's Thursday midnight, and the youth are on the streets -

> **GIRL**
> We've been to t' Crazy Daisy. It weren't too bad. We do like Roxy Music. We like Soul, us.
> **BOY**
> Where you going back to?
> **GIRL**
> Us husbands is waiting at home for us.
> **ANOTHER GIRL**
> We was in Scamps. It seemed that everybody there were all same.

---

122 Ray Ashcroft, Christine Cox, Alwyne Taylor and David Boyce, with Rex Doyle producing.

GIRL
There was nobody that had a personality of their own.
ANOTHER GIRL
Yes that's it.
GIRL
Everybody's same.

At seven minutes to three in the morning, table tennis is being played at the GPO as a post office worker gets angry at having to go round posting giros for people who make more than he does by being out of work. He's voting Tory next time, he says, and -

GPO WORKER
I keep telling the kids - get some qualifications. You mustn't end up like me.

Glad's van runs out of bacon, opposite Tommy Wards.

Pearl's a Singer is on the commercial radio on the hour through the night.

A woman unpacks newspapers and says she'll be praying for everybody in Sheffield and all around Sheffield tonight, at Endcliffe Methodists, with eleven others.

Arnold Dodd sets off to work explaining why he's a socialist -

ARNOLD
Quite honestly I find it incredible to think a working bloke would vote bloody Conservative. It's something I can't bloody stomach, that. I can't see his bloody logic in voting bloody Conservative. He bloody knows what bloody kind of bloody people they bloody are.

Only he doesn't say *bloody*.

Posh kids in Broomhill talk Latin on their way to school. Sarah has a birthday. And Ray Ashcroft re-enacts his secretly-taped bollocking.

BANK MANAGER
Have a seat, Mr Ashcroft. Now then what's happened to this current account then?

A gambler backs Willie Carson.

There's a strike at the *Telegraph and Star*.

116

An off-licence lady tells of the sybarites of North East Derbyshire -

OFF LICENCE LADY
They eat cheese and sausages and what-have-you and they make punch and things like that. We do an awful lot of parties in Dronfield!

The company sing a punky song -

Would you like a dream house in Dronfield
Far from life's battles and never to roam?
Far from the hassle
Your Englishman's castle?
A dream house in Dronfield and all on your own?
How much else do we need to show you?
By your dreams we shall know you!

A Chilean refugee talks about concentration camps, as a waitress dreams of a white wedding -

WAITRESS
Good I don't earn much, won't miss it when I give up work.

A woman is sad about her mother -

WOMAN
I wish you could help me mother instead of talking. I'll just have to make the most of it while she's still here.

A kid from Herries is sad about the stereo -

PUPIL
We go up Colley youth club some nights. It's rubbish, boring. The stereo's busted. The telly's busted. It's just table tennis and cards. And I'm no good at cards.

A crook tells Vera in Netherthorpe her nearside front wheel's nearly off, takes money from her to buy new ball bearings, and disappears.

We go into Wadsley Asylum-as-was, while just up the road Jane Elizabeth Andrew, aged six, is crowned Wadsley-as-is's May Queen.

JANE
I would like to thank everyone who has helped with the May Day and I 'ope…hope… you have a very happy evening as we entertain you.

Basset's sweet workers do all sorts all night.

We cut between a German beer cellar, and a homeless shelter.

The narration tells us there have been 25 fire incidents during the day and the cook at Mansfield Park Fire Station has retired after 37 years.

Oh, and a woman has accused her neighbour of fancying her, and not telling his wife.

More people have been born than have died, so that's all right. And Nan, although she'll fail to make the meeting, has agreed to do her egg and cress anyway.

*

Theatre companies should do new verbatim plays every year in every Main House of every theatre in Britain. Let the people speak, say I.

> *As a political dramatist Robinson lacks the Brechtian ability to hold his fire.*
> Tim Brown (Telegraph)

Little Claudine Tadier
or
Waiting For The Muscadet To Turn Red

To All In Tents was a play I wrote for the Young Vic in London that tried to celebrate Plevenon, which is a tiny village in Brittany, not far from the St Malo ferry, where we had cycled for our first Abroad, in 1959.

Such *amis* and *amies* we were there – Mimi and Pierre, Gerard, Klaus, Edmonde, Dolores, Malcolm K, Sandra, Seamus, Dave, Dave in his pyjamas, Miles, Geoff and June, the art teacher, the other art teacher, the German girl, the Dutch girl with glasses, the old communist Bernard Plasseraud, Alan, and George Donaldson. And Jacques, Ceinwen, Jenny, Jacko, Jean Jacques, Norman, Mary, Francine, Daniel and Jean Paul and Marie Paul Bulot and Gerard Frite, and Gerard Guegeniat, M Dubois and Madame Herve, and Linda, and Henri and Henri Barbier, Daniel, Daniel and Danielle, and little Claudine Tadier giggling in her glasses as she served on in the *alimentation*.

We'd biked there in 1959 to the *Auberge de la Jeunesse* and went back there every wet summer for years - camping, hostelling, anythinging, and always hoping the weather would get better, and the Muscadet would turn red, and we'd never get any older.

We played tennis and boules, swam in the calvados sea, and half-cooked whole sheep we'd nearly killed ourselves.

We slurred *Chevaliers de la Table Ronde*, about the man who died with his head under the wine tap-

> *Goutons voir si le vin est bon!*
> *Goutons voir oui oui oui!*
> *Goutons voir non non non!*

We cockled, spoke Whitmarsh, hoped for more women on bikes, enjoyed kermesses and accordion dance bands on Sundays and fest noz's in fields of mist.

We chanted round cheminees, and, especially in 1968, sang *The Internationale* like they were singing it in Paris, though our French comrades in Brittany preferred to shout about roast beef -

> *Et merde a la reigne d' angleterre!*

I wrote a *Song of the Tents* to celebrate the evenements -

> *The German in the caravan*
> *He's doing fine*
> *One French au pair and one fraulein*
> *See him neath his awning*
> *Bow legged in the morning*
> *He's getting his share*
> *Who's getting mine?*

And many verses later -

> *So come on campers you all know it's time*
> *Something something something ime*
> *Get up off your asses*
> *And screw the ruling classes*
> *They're getting their share plus yours and mine*
> *They're getting their share plus yours and mine!*

Only when we got on the ferry in late August 68, and read our first Daily Express for a month, did we get the news of the invasion of Czechoslovakia.[123]

To All In Tents at the Young Vic in London was about all that.

But it was the summer, and nobody came, except the papers.

> *Clever clever title.*
> The Stage

> *Feebly-entitled but occasionally amusing new comedy set in a campsite on the coast of Brittany in the summer of 1968. The period is established with debatable accuracy by the incidental soundtrack of contemporary records and also with heavy-handed insistence by the script's repeated reference to the fact. 'It's 1968' one character points out more than once.*
> The Times

---

123 We did get older. And, with kids, we went to Greece for yellow wine and sunshine. But when we flew back to Brittany, though not all of us, in May 2008, most of Plevenon was still there. Fort La Latte was. And Cap Frehel. And the ugly church, and the lavs, though with seats now. And the beaches. And the skies. And chocolat chaud, rain and cartes postale. The boulangerie smelt the same too. Little Claudine Tadier was still there giggling in her glasses, though the alimentation was empty. And she was the Mayor.

Awkward gear changes. Apparently unexceptional scenario.... a brittle edge, which just relieves this predominantly light-hearted piece from mediocrity.
The Guardian

Mrs Turner's Arthur

Jokers was a trilogy of cheap didactic dialect dialectic shows that Paul Allen[124] and I wrote for the *Crucible* in the 1980s.

> *The acclaimed and cultish saga set somewhere equidistant from the Don, The Dearne, and the Rother. The latest dollop of South Yorkshire mythology with housewife-nearly-superstar Rita May.*
> Crucible publicity

We called it soap but the actors made it better than that.

Some people still ask if there's ever going to be another episode. I don't think we could beat Christine Cox's Julie in her bride's outfit, and Norman Mills' Young Arthur Turner in his Santa costume, clutching each other just before she marries somebody else.

Chuffs.

---

124 Vicar's son, Oxford classicist, trade unionist, trombonist, critic, broadcaster, beardie, beer lover, a bit of a fussy man, and yet another of my friends with an amazing wife. We've shared shabby digs and shabby friends for most of our grown-up lives. He's good when you're in trouble, and has done more unpaid work to help the arts round here than anyone.

Mike and Flee

Flee and Mike are the names I gave my former partner Viv Thom[125] and me in two two-handed plays about starting a family, written when we were starting a family ourselves.

Holding the Baby was on the London fringe, and tells the tale of two ex-teachers who find they are having a baby not-quite-by-mistake.[126]

They squabble from pregnancy test to birth, but we leave them choosing names in bed and looking forward to happy endings.

> **FLEE**
> I love you.
> **MIKE**
> Love is what people yell at each other across no man's land to tempt each other into the barbed wire.

Our radical midwife recommended the play to her customers. The reviews were pally. The audiences laughed and stayed behind to talk and say funny how you forget, but it was like that wasn't it?

Then I wrote *Child's Play*, and it's Mike and Flee 18 months later, on the night when, terminally sleepless, they've changed their minds about how awful it is to leave babies crying in the dark, and are about to do just that for three nights, as recommended by Spock.

They sit up by their tightly-made bed waiting for their baby to cry in the other room so that they can then not go in to him. To pass the time, they rip each other up.

> **FLEE**
> He's a new human being. We should be ashamed of the world as it is.

---

125 Ramsgate, Dorking. Mother a teacher. Father in the NHS. We met after she was recruited straight from the Labour Exchange the day before term to work at Sedgehill School in the Social Education Department, which was where all the kids with real difficulties were ghettoed. I was still teaching sex and English there, but was about to run away to join the theatre. She stayed in London, worked in FE, and at the Women's Centre in Deptford. We were on/off for years, till Goronwy was born, and then we came up to Sheffield. She taught at Castle and then Hallam Uni. We had three kids, and I probably wouldn't have had any if we hadn't, certainly not those three, so that was good. And three cats but no dog. She once bought me a soft felt plectrum for playing the Autoharp silently, and once saved my life.
126 David Learner from RADA was better at being me than I was.

MIKE
Perhaps we shouldn't have invited him into it then.
FLEE
He isn't going to be brought up like we were.
MIKE
He is being.

The audiences stayed behind to talk again, even when they should have been off home to relieve their babysitters.

My dear friend from Keble and London, Dave Wasp, wrote me a letter -

> *I don't really like it much…grossly sentimental and a step back … Hasty… so easy…What were these two people trying to say to me? What possible interest is there in it for me?...Extend yourself as a writer…It's time to write a real play and stop wanking about.*[127]

It was the first play to be directed by Clare Venables the new Crucible Director, and she nearly took Mike and Flee to the Royal Court, where she was well known. But I sold them to the BBC instead.

*

Child's Play wasn't the first time I'd used Viv Thom and me in stories, though rarely so close to our bones. It felt like a compliment - fancy us being important enough to be written about! Fancy us being so *zeitgeisty!* Look at what happening to us! Laugh! Learn! Move on!

When Viv did move on, and left me, I wrote about that too, and put us into the long comic story I was writing. Everyone said it ruined it. And that's why in these memoirs I've left lots of her out. We did our best for our twenty odd years, more or less. Our kids are brilliant. That'll do.

*

But Mike and Flee?

Might there be more of them?

Has Flee flown?

---

127 My Megan read this and was shocked, asked to see the original letter and thought that I should also include the bit where Dave also says, 'Someone holding himself back and showing glimpses of great talent…I want to be able to go to the theatre unaided when you do [write a real play].' I wonder what he'll say about this book, though?

Or, thirty-odd years on, are they still together?

Still mistaking *struggle* for *love?*

Still wondering why men can't be a bit less useless? And women a bit less of a bother?

And where jokes fit in? And kids?

And if the personal is still political? And what love's got to do with it?

Will Mike and Flee *(m and f)* still be spending too much time wondering what's gone wrong for it ever to go right?

Wondering if they ever liked each other?

And if - oh the big question – it would have been better if they'd never met?[128]

> **MIKE**
> I always thought I'd get pregnant.
> **FLEE**
> So did I. And once I did.
> **MIKE**
> And I wasn't there.
> **FLEE**
> I should have asked.
> **MIKE**
> I'm glad you didn't.

*

By the time of *Child's Play,* I was back living in Sheffield with Viv and baby Goronwy[129] and, almost without noticing, had stopped being itinerant and had joined the grown ups - which is exactly what Mike was so scared of in the plays.

During the run, *Sheffielder* from the *Star* came round as part of the Crucible's publicity push for their surprise hit show. He turned out to be Stephen McClarence, my Mum's star pupil from Sharrow Lane. He ate heartily at my

---

128 No. I'd have been two plays short. (When my Megan read this footnote, she said to miss out the second sentence)
129 Goronwy Matthew Guy Robinson Thom.

expense and wrote a wintry piece called *A Nappy Family* that exactly caught us all at a strange time. I asked if I could use it in these memoirs and he said he'd rather not, he thought he'd been unfair.

I told him he is a mardybum.

But he can't stop you looking up the *Stars* of January 1982.

And reading this -

> *You might say that millions of people manage to have children without agonising traumatically about it. But that would only be your opinion.*

> *Well to be honest it would be my opinion as well.*

And this -

> *Goronwy slept peacefully through it all.*

Making It Up On Fridays

The Friday Show in the mid-eighties was maybe the most interesting theatrical thing that happened round here in our lifetimes.

Maybe.

What did happen was that on Friday nights there was this show at the Leadmill, for lovers of theatre and for anyone else who fancied getting into the disco cheaper by coming to the *Friday Show* first.

And it was open access -

> *Watch it Friday night! Be in it Saturday afternoon!*

The following were among those involved - Debbie Egan, Chris Wilkinson, Adrian Vinkin, Bill Paton, the Roland Millers, Benji Ming, Chris Meade, Trudge - and me.

The usual.

Nobody got paid.

As usual.

There were songs, plays, site-specifics,[130] avant-gardes, bricollages, socialisms, realisms, anarchisms, high art, low art, and shakeitallabout art, plus Betty Spital, music, lights, acting, dance, satire, revue, living newspapers, poems, stunts, feminism, circus and godknowswhat.

Such optimism! Create a complex show with a different theme each week, with a new set and new costumes and new music, in five part-time days with a big cast that anybody can join and leave whenever they want!

Make it up in a week, chuck it away after one performance!

Subsidised theatre companies should do *Friday Shows* every week. Let the people show off, say I.

Some of our showing-off was bit wonderful. All gone now. Except - there is still £457 in a *Friday Show* Co-Op bank account, and I know who's got the keys.

---

130 One whole show seemed to take place above the men's lavs.

7. The Best Day Of Their Lives

My Comeback

17 Woodland Place was a clumsy half house, on the steep road that suddenly swoops you up from Queen Victoria, out of Totley off to Bradway, and the World.

It cost £24K in 1981 and was the first property I've ever owned even half of a half of.

Viv, baby Goronwy and I had no work, and the £8K down payment on it came from three jammy Christmas shows I'd just done.

The original Edwardian house had been clumsily spliced in the 1930s, with little bits built on. The people next door had to get down into their cellar via a trap door in the middle of their front room, and once they did they usually found they were in ours.

The garage was on street level at the front but was suddenly perched on a tumbling hillside at the back. There were wonky leaded windows at the front with wonky sills. The French door at the back opened onto a precipice of little paths, lawns and rockeries, all the way to the posh trees at the end of the posh houses at the bottom coming up the other way.

Everything sloped - floors, doors, cupboards, walls and gardens.

Everything was a bit damp and a bit rotting and there was a lake under the lounge when the floorboards gave way.

There was a 1930's square brick extension that jutted out at the back. This had a tiny square room filled with books and theatre posters where tiny Goronwy and I rang the bell on my portable Olivetti, and made up stories, overlooking our valley.

There was a tiny square kitchen below, filled with tables, sinks, demijohns, nappy buckets, homebrew beer buckets, pinboards and buggies.

The biggest bedroom from the old house was in our half but it wasn't very big and was itself three-quartered, to make another bedroom through a cardboard wall, for Goronwy not to sleep in.

The bathroom was shiny black and yellow art deco.

Viv added a steep aluminium ladder to get into a secret roof, where relatives could be hidden. There was a real willow weeping in the front garden and beyond it a real island in the middle of the roads.

We bought it all from Christine, a classmate from All Saints School. I'd been to a long-ago party of hers in Totley Bents and in a barn had kissed her little sister, who tasted of bilberry, but I've never told.

My Mum and Dad were four and a half minutes down the hill from No 17, by buggy.[131]

It was wonderful to be home, with my own little boy. I'm still grateful to Viv for coming. I'd got back the rivers and woods I'd had 40 years before, with the up-Manx trains still chuffing up my valley into my moors.

*

Eleanor Rose Robinson Thom[132] was born just after our fourth Christmas, on the floor of the big bedroom overlooking the island beyond the willow that weeps no more.

The frost on all our sloping hedges was never frostier than at sunrise on that most wonderful of mornings.

Goronwy planned to watch the actual birth but when push came to shove he was more into Postman Pat doing his own delivering downstairs.

*

I was unemployed, then self-employed, then sort-of-employed at the Crucible. Viv got a job at Granville College. Then the BBC took me on daily for a bit (or as it turned out for ever). We could now borrow even more money we couldn't afford, and because No 17 couldn't get any bigger with all its leaning and sloping, we bought 132 Totley Brook Road from Bill Moore, the working class history man, for £34K. I knew him too, and again that helped, both of us.

---

131 The night my Dad died I was with my Mum in one and a half.
132 Goronwy's five names (with 29 letters in them, for a boy born on the 29th August, which is also Edward Carpenter's birthday) took three months to agree. Viv chose all Eleanor's names. We stalemated on Megan Aphra, and I sort of lost because I wanted her the other way round if she was going to be a feminist theatrical. (And she was). I didn't want any of them to have my surname because I am a feminist theatrical too, but I sneaked it back in on the taxi ride to Goronwy's registrar.

When we moved out of No 17 the removal men cut the bulbs off the lights, untuned the piano and broke as much as they could, so we never paid them.

And then we were living in another tumbly half house, with more rooms than we could count, with a new cat, new baby - and 17 years to go.

Me

South Yorkshire's favourite uncle who everyone seems to trust.[133]
Dean Pepall (Yorkshire Post Nov 16th, 1998)

Dear John
I like you please can you write back to me. love Timothyxxxxxx
Timothy writing to his uncle,[134] c1976

---

133 Does that 'seems to' seem a bit dodgy?
134 Cf Uncle Timothy who was in the Telegraph c1950. My Dad knew Uncle Timothy because of the Freemasons, but he didn't know Aunt Edith from The Star. I always confused Aunt Edith with Aunt Fanny from the Famous Five, which also had a Timothy in it, though I was always George. And Timothy my nephew became Tim, c1985, anyway.

My Day Out In Rotherham

I'm not sure if it was the X4. Or the1305.

But I do know when and where I had the best idea of my life.

I was going to do a one-off class with some drama students at Rotherham College for the usual negligible fee minus tax and NI.

The *Red Ladder Theatre* in Leeds had rung up as I was leaving home to ask if by any chance I'd got a play or anything with a very small cast? Northern? No rock music? Something comic? One-night stands at working men's clubs in six weeks' time? Well five actually? Lose the grant if something wasn't done fast? Need a title at least? Help?

I said course, ring you back, got to go to Rotherham.

*

I'd already written one show for *Red Ladder* about a Circus, and it included the *Great Whitby Magic Escape Box,* demonstrating how the workers would soon break free from capitalism. It wasn't that magic, and we couldn't always get it up the stairs at venues, especially if they wanted bingo as well. But I loved the company, and the ideas behind the Company, trotting away in their crumbly back-to-back chapel in Leeds where they made their good-natured plans for the Revolution.

*

So here I am jolting on the 1305 X4 through what's left of the steel industry, trying to think of a title, and wondering how to write a new play in a couple of days. Or better, how to re-jig an old one without anyone noticing.

And I remember Burton-on-Trent.

I went there a few years ago by train, to interview this woman in a bungalow about the night she saw the lone German airman who blitzed Rolls Royce at Derby, and waved.

By ten past ten I'd taped her twice, eaten her scones, and was marooned in Burton till teatime. But, on my way to see her, I'd noticed an advert for a *Bass Museum.* It might do till the Bass pubs opened?

Robinsons at the seaside in c 1930

Me uncombed

As Buttons

The Oxford cartoon by the future Times cartoonist Frank Whitford

Cherwell 1963

Robinsons at the seaside c 1964

Me teaching at my comprehensive 1968

Me and Capstick on a hill 1980s

Me, Sally, Maisie 2008

My Eleanor as a baby, photo by me

My Megan as an actor, photo by Goronwy

My Goronwy as a juggler

Robinsons at the seaside 2009

Me at a 21- bar Appalachian Autoharp

And it did do, because, in addition to dry displays of brewing through the ages, there was a bookstall with various replicas from the great days of beer. And one of the replicas was of a booklet given to each Bass beer worker who went on the firm's day trip to Scarborough, ten days before the outbreak of the First World War.

I'd flicked through it at the bookstall.

From 2am, it said, a dozen special trains took the brewery workers, at ten-minute intervals off to the seaside. The lowliest workers left earliest, and came home soonest. The bosses stayed the week. The booklet told the workers how to behave, and what there was to see in Scarborough that was educational, and how not to miss the train home, or in any other way bring the good name of beer into disrepute.

I'd bought the Bass booklet, to show willing, then dived into some Bass pubs, and probably taken it home, wherever home was then.

So anyway here I am now on the X4 approaching Rotherham and starting to scribble.

Brewery outing
Beer
Trains
Bathing Machines
Whatshisface the Whitby photographer
High tides on Marine Drive

I do the session with the students, scribbling while they act up.

Sets off from Sheffield?
Bossy boss.
Humble workers
A Leftie who stands up to them (Like the communist I worked with at
the concrete firm Frazzis when I was 17?)

I scribble on on the X4 again.

Underground pleasure garden
The Pyjama Game
Peaseholme Park (How do you spell it?)

I scribble in Pond Street waiting for the 24.

Open top trams
Bathing machines
Middle aged couple
Will they dare stay overnight?
Include Dad's song 4 and 9 – not too 30s?
Call it Britling's beer? H.G.Wells?

I scribble on the 24.

When was War declared?
Didn't beer get rationed?
The Sitwells?
Spa open-air bandstand
What the Butler Saw
A painter in the brewery who also paints watercolours
Italian ice cream - but whose side were the Italians on in that war?
First world war poetry
Beer and sunshine

By the time I get home, I've a notebookful of scribble - including three scribbled suffragettes who are going to have such a day out without men, and two pals called Spud and Dusty who love beer and each other, like Spud and Dusty from *The Plume of Feathers* in the days of the Maze Hill Commune. And a spinster from the brewery office who hopes her male friend will ask her to miss the return train and -

I chase up to my bookshelves, and chuck books around.

I find maps of the East Coast.

An old diary.

The Outing by Dylan Thomas.

A Ward Locke *Scarborough* guide.

Blakemore's *Yorkshire Wit.*

The Ragged Trousered Philanthropists.

And… the Bass booklet! Still here! Waiting patiently for its outing.

*

136

Someone else gives the kids tea, bath and bed.

Or doesn't.

God has come home. I'm creating.

*

By 7 o'clock in the morning, I'd written my *Beano* - or done everything but.

I had the title, plot, the characters, the names, the setting, the history, the song, and the beginnings of a language I could write it in.

I rang *Red Ladder* and said I had this play that -

They said yes but what's the title?

I said very small cast, no rock music, fairly comic, Northern, could easily do one-night stands at working men's clubs, just needed to fair-copy it, soon as it was type -?

Yes but what's it called? We've got to get the funding and the posters sorted.

What about like, well - *The Beano?*

They said great title! Open in Grimsby, five weeks.

*

My Dad died three days before Grimsby, which made Norman Mills' rendition of 4 and 9 hard.

> *I took a girl out West one night*
> *She had a very fine appetite.* [135]

*

The tour of *Red Ladder's Beano* was a gas. Every performance was like a day out. We drank too much, flirted, befriended strangers, spent up,

---

[135] The last wonderful thing my wonderful Dad did for me was to phone round all his old pals to reconstruct the words and tune of 4 and 9 for me to use in The Beano.

had holiday romances, went to funny places, cried every night about Miss Tidmarsh and Mr Shepherd from the office, and didn't want to go home when it was over any more than the workers did.

No one noticed how much of *The Beano* I'd pinched from *The Ragged Trousered Philanthropists,* including the title, which is what Tressell called his Chapter 44 about the bosses' treat, when the workers are filled up with free beer and become grateful and patriotic, while the hero Owen thinks how hard it will be to ever change things.

I'd even named my hero *Owen* in *hommage.*

*

For the next 10 years *The Beano* was me.

There were stage plays, musicals, a film (nearly), the novel, the American novel, the paperback, the Book of Beanos, the Radio 4 epic, lectures, five different student versions, an opera, and all the readings and talks.

It's the writing I enjoyed most ever (except this book), and the only idea to come complete, at one go.

And the only writing of mine I can still read now.

We still go to Scarborough, sometimes, to remember what we've done for five generations -

> *Children's Corner*
> *Ayckbourn*
> *The bookies*
> *Corrigans*
> *The Cumberland*
> *The Astoria*
> *The waffles*
> *Aerial warfare*
> *The Spa*
> *The Harbour Bar*
> *The Villa Esplanade*
> *The Highlander*
> *The lift*

But when we do go there, I also remember, and can nearly see, little gangs of beer workers drinking their own beer, and three suffragettes-for-the-day, and Comrade Owen still hoping for the best, all in Edwardian costume having the times of all their lives all the summer's day long.

And I remember Rotherham[136] too, and the magical mystery tour that started for me on that 1305 X4, if that's what it was, on the day I set off on all my Beanos without knowing where they'd end.

> *The Beano is terrific. I think you have done everything that I had hoped and probably much more. The book is highly entertaining, immensely vivid and yet rather poignantly in a not too cloyingly nostalgic way. Comparisons with Under Milk Wood are not inappropriate, it seems to me. So many congratulations.*
> Robert McCrum of Faber, now Observer literary editor.

> *Rony Robinson shares with Dylan Thomas a gift for caricature, and a sharp and poetic eye, ear and nose for the sights and smells of imaginary worlds that we all recognise as anything but imaginary.*
> Peter Danville (The Times)

> *Like a plebeian Under Milk Wood it tried to be larger than life and say things like, 'Listen with a flick of a seagull's claw the silence ends!' To be fair some of it was considerably better than that but it did seem interminable.*
> Paul Ferris (The Observer)

---

136 I think Steve McClarence, the journalist who was unhelpful with the Star piece from 1982, did his initial courting of his now wife Clare Jenkins, and made his first unambiguous moves (or she did) on the same bus journey. Maybe even on the same bus. I wouldn't have noticed.

139

My Day Out In Sheffield

On Friday July 24 1987 Sheffield Central Libraries were turned into the seaside, under the slogan *Libraries Are So Bracing*.

There were donkeys in Surrey Street. Musicians made real music in the Music Library.

There were *What the Butler Saw* machines in the Reference Library, puppets and ice cream in the Children's Library and Dilly the Musical Pierrot on a beach.

There were also Deputy Lord Mayors, t-shirts, a jazz band, kiss-me-quick hats, a ghost train in the library cellars, Madam Zelda, sticks of rock, a bandstand, busloads of Sheffield holidaymakers, radio, TV, the papers, and Tony Capstick singing about Punch and Judy.

It was a huge celebration of *The Beano* that had just been published by Faber. I got the day off work, and we all had a wonderful time.

*

The Chief Librarian spoke to the holidaymakers about how important writers and holidays are.

I was allowed to sit in a deckchair reading aloud in the very middle of the library.

I watched my own book getting its plastic cover and its extra page for stamping the date on, and then being put on the shelves with all the other books ever written, free for ever like them.

We tea-danced in the classical music library and drank wine by the Outsize Books.

My Mum cried because she was so happy and sad.

Me too.

My Goronwy, Eleanor and Megan were all so young, and we were about to go for a week's big holiday in Scarborough ourselves, to spend and swim and hopscotch and bury each other, in the sandy footprints of my brewery workers, down the Spa and along to the Harbour and off on the open-tops to Peasholme.

We didn't know, any more than the 1914 brewery workers did, how little time was left.

But if that bracing July day wasn't the best day of all their lives, and ours, it did to be going on with.[137]

---

137 And there was a sequel. The Beano had a baby. Clare Jenkins from the previous footnote, and her pals, went round the library shelves all day on July 24, collecting people's stories of their own works outings and she later produced the wonderful Bumper Book of Beanos about real working Sheffielders at play.

May I Make A Suggestion?

You may find it more interesting to read, say, the experiences of a sex education teacher in an inner-city comp?

Turn back and read it then.

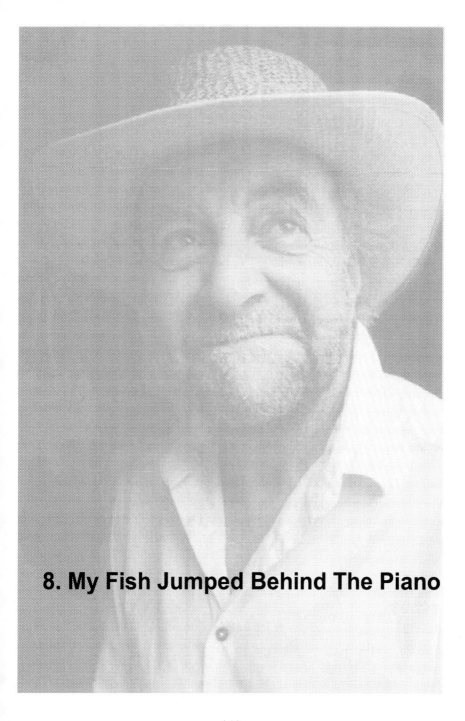

8. My Fish Jumped Behind The Piano

One Three Two

When we moved into 132 Totley Brook Road we were a mummy, a daddy, a five-year-old and a baby.[138]

132 was a tumbly four-or-five-storey Victorian semi with a long thin garden at the back, facing the wrong way for the sun, five minutes from the *Crown*, with King Ecgbert over the garden wall, and trees and countryside and moors everywhere. And there was a secret path via the Akky to Totley, with the Derbyshire river you could always hear.

It was just the place to live happy ever after at.

*

It was ramshackle when we moved in, and ramshackle when we left.

In between it was mostly ramshackle.

It had so many rooms it didn't know what to do.

Viv changed every one of them, except the garage, and that was never a garage anyway. It was a theatre for a bit, with tip-up real theatre seats. It was a wine cellar too, and a coal cellar, and a bikes, meter, wardrobe, freezer, saws, boxes and rammel cellar. All it ever did was need sorting.

On the ground floor there was a thin hall with a CND sticker declaring in black and white on the inside of the real Victorian front door under the real Victorian glass -

> *This is a peace house.*

There was a dartboard on the door at the end of the thin hall. On the right there were two side-by-side stripped knobbly doors that didn't shut, and led into the same room anyway. That room with its partition that never partitioned, overlooked Totley Brook Road, one storey up, and had a fat window shelf for cushions and cats.

That room is where the big table was with its secret middle bit, for writing, gameplaying, drinking, jigsawing, nappychanging, cat defleaing, puppet showing, reading, dossing, eating and playing happy families on.[139]

---

138 I asked my daughter Megan when I was writing this bit what she'd want to say about 132. She said horsy horsy and the mummers and the promenade plays we did all round the house and garden.

139 Jill Hnat lent it to us 25 years ago. Viv painted it light green and distressed it so she wouldn't want it back. I am typing these memoirs on it now, up in my writing attic, and hope Jill

Also in this two-in-one room was the clunking old Aga, warm and alive till the day before we left.

The ceilings were high enough to juggle under, and there was a proscenium arch for shows.

Here was where almost everything that happened happened, except for sleeping and the telly.

The piano was kept open ready for *horsy horsy,* which was when someone played -

> *duddle um*
> *duddle um*
> *duddle um dum um*

and when anyone we loved could get the horse from the cellar and gallop round in different hats -

> *duddle um*
> *duddle um*
> *duddle um dum um.*

We played *bugger-off* [140] here too.

There was a thin French door at the far end. It never shut, and led into a tiny sunless conservatory with nothing to conserve except the conservatory table on which Megan and Eleanor played their game of *CT.* [141]

Turn left out through two clicky doors that weren't worth closing, and there was a small windowless room with a real fireplace and the telly with the bust scart lead. And the stained stripy three-piece suite, on the stained light green carpet that was always a mistake.

---

doesn't remember this bit of our past and want her table back when we meet for the launch of this book at the Totley History Group. (And I hope she doesn't buy this book if she does. Or if she does I hope she doesn't read the footnotes. Or remembers, if she does, it's all for charity.)

140 What that was, you had to keep catching the beanbag one-handed. But you could only move when the other person had it. Just before you threw each time you had to say 'Bugger-off!' If you didn't, you had to go back to the front door again. You had to do that if you dropped it as well. Or if you used two hands. But if you didn't, you could keep going till you got all the way to the back of the house, and then you had to flop it in the hat, and you won, only we were all winners at our house.

141 Conservatory Table.

Off that, without a door, was another room, without a name, then the outside lav only the window cleaner was allowed to use, and a shed full of slug pellets, wine equipment and saws. It had a bendy shelf of logs, for Goronwy to camp out on, and whitewashed bricks for him to write graffiti on, about the Tories and Yazoo.

On the first floor there was a bathroom with bath, lav, bidet, washing machine and dryer behind the funny shuttery doors, and a shower, if you could find it. There was no lock, and someone always came in to talk and read and sing.

Then three bedrooms.

The first was Goronwy's, with its theatrical dressing room mirror. Megan Aphra Robinson Thom was born here in the middle of an August afternoon that tasted of damsons and warm herb cheese. Goronwy and Eleanor, that birth day, preferred to go swimming in Dronfield with Tracey.[142]

Then there was Eleanor's room with its mezzanine bed and playhouse, and the ceilingful of stars at bedtime to read *Winnie the Pooh* by, for ever.

Then Viv's box room. And up the wooden stairs to a thin attic office full of books and me. Then two more bedrooms - Megan's full of stories, cuddlies and shelves of tiny secret things, and then the mummy and daddy room with its view of the Akky,[143] just.

So what's that? Fifteen rooms? Sixteen?

Plus Megan's cupboard, that was at least half a room, because sometimes Bert the Squirt the plumber had to climb up it to get under the roof into the secret village hall at the top of both houses.

Outside at the back there were vast hedges to keep out our through-the-wall neighbours John and Bessie, and their yappy likely dogs Bob and Terry, and their smelly hens.

---

142 Tracey, Siobhan and Belinda did a lot of the early childcare. They loved us, and were loved back, and made all our lives easier.

143 The Akky is a bridge that has carried the Old Hay Brook over the Manchester train line since 1894. I could just see it for twenty years from the mummy and daddy room when I leaned out looking for the badgers and courting couples squeaking in the hill of trees on the other side of the railway. People do things in the Akky because they think they can't be seen. Goronwy said local lads took steroids there. Eleanor and Megan swam naked in it when nobody was looking. (They never swam in it again though people were looking all the time). Maisie loves the slopey red and black bricks and the clean Derbyshire water when we cross it at low tide in sunny Augusts. I've fallen in it three times so far, starting at the age of six.

Between the huge hedges were an orchard, a pond, swings, vegetable beds, a Yorkshire stone patio in different pastels for our own version of hopscotch, and a shed at the end with electricity that could be switched on or off, depending on whether you wanted an exhibition, or somewhere to misbehave.

> *Roger and Rosemary up a tree*
> *Roger and Rosemary up a tree*

Roger and Rosemary were our neighbours over the hedge on the right, facing King Ecgbert. Roger had ginger and snow whiskers, and then just snow. Rosemary still collects for St Luke's and still pretends to laugh when Maisie still pretends to bite her. They loved their terrier Sooty as much as we loved our terrier Maisie but they didn't love each other.[144]

> *Roger and Rosemary up a tree*
> *Doing something naughty!*

I don't think they ever did go up a tree together.[145]

There was table tennis on the second lawn, by the gooseberries and blackcurrants, under the apples. At the far end of the garden there were fat ancient trees, a dry stone wall, the gate into next door, and then playing fields for ever, until we were all PFI'd and turned to concrete.

132 was a dusty, artlessly arty house, with its stripped knobble and bidet, framed piano certificates, autoharps, pictures of Bob Dylan, chalk boards, pinboards, dart boards, wooden floors, real fires, stoves, unmatching frames with photos, posters and slogans.

No stripped knobbly doors ever shut, and everyone said it was too draughty, especially when you lounged on the fading William Morris chesterfield under the fading William Morris curtains drooping down the front windows.

The house smelt of wine, cooking, babies, fruit, fires, and crayons.

There were books, and musical instruments and circus stuff, and homework, diaries, clothes, letters, food, bottles and – clutter, rammel and tranquelments[146] everywhere, comfortingly always still there, however often you had to tidy up.

*

---

144 The dogs, that is.

145 Roger and Rosemary, that is.

146 You spell it then.

The people who moved in after us were a mummy and daddy with a five-year-old and a baby.

> *There I met a monkey*
> *Just like me*

It is just the place to live happy ever after at.

I hope they are doing.[147]

---

147 A bloke who read this commented that this whole section is too happy to be true.

Not Forgetting

My Mum wrote little Collins red-and-black page-a-day diaries for decades.

She started when Dave first went off to sea, so that she could remember what to tell him in her weekly letters. She wanted her diaries burning after, but I have them crammed in the bookcase above me as I write this.

*

Geth wrote diaries for years, always weeks behind, mainly recording his scores at Newfooty, tennis and golf.

He destroyed them all in a *King Lear* cleanout in his early 60s.

*

At King Edward's I kept two foolscap Boots diaries, cross-indexed with successful jokes and reading lists, and asterixes indicating nocturnal emissions. I did a couple of journals at Oxford, and one when first teaching in London.

They are unobservant and self-centred even for diaries but I've never destroyed them in case I ever needed to remember what it was like to be me then.

*

Dad and Dave were never keen on doing any writing they could avoid, so no diaries for them.

*

But then, not long after Eleanor was born, we began to do page-a-day A 4 hardback family diaries, two a year, for ever.

Into them went anything that we could stick, staple, rip, fold, paste, draw or list. Anyone who came round had to write stories and songs and poems and true things and pretend things, and draw and stick and paste what they wanted as well, even if they didn't want.

Someone with grown-up kids had suggested it was great way of not forgetting family things that mattered.

I keep all those family diaries in an upstairs cupboard, and try not to look at them on my own. (I've done the pinching of stuff for this book on my own though, and felt a bit prurient doing it, sometimes.)

Other One Is Burst

Secretly stuck into the family diary instead of going up the chimney c1985.

Goronwy
Totley County School
Totley Sheffield

7th December

Dear father Christmas

I would like a film called the Blues Brothers because it is a good film. And some compute games because I have got a computer. I would like the new Sheffield Wednesday Kit because I like Sheffield Wednesday. And some football boots because I like playing football could I also have some Sheffield Wednesday shin pads because you mite get hurt. And a Sheffield Wednesday. football because my other one is burst.

Your sincerely goronwy Thom xxxxxxxxx

Octa

Goronwy writes in His Marks and Spencer Book *This is Me With Questions and Stickers,* forever now stuck in the family diary for 1987.

This book belongs to Goronwy
I am 6 years old.
The first word I said as a baby was Octa.
My favourite joke is How do you weigh a whale? Go to a whale way station!
My father likes drinking. My mother likes having a rest.
I have a pet called Dinah and Hue and Tom. It is a cat and two fish. It likes to eat fish food or Kite cat. It is 2 and 1 years old. It lives in a house. My cat stays out all day and all night and my fish jump behind the piano. The End.
The present I got for my last birthday were a whistle, and a stone with a hole in it that said words.
My favourite pop stars are Tracy Chapman.
My favourite records are fast car and across the lines.
The job I would like to do is act. I would like to do this because I like them.
If I could have a perfect day I would choose to spend it on drinks.

O Mr Stacky!
From the family diaries 1990.

Stacky was a caretaker[148] at Eleanor and Megan's school and, in the stories, took tea on his flat roof with Mrs H, on her way home, and sometimes helped her search for spare bones in the Dore Church graveyard.

He was also involved in the curly tale of *The Bride Wore Brown*, who sat veiled and eager on the front upstairs seat of the 50 Dore bus, looking forward to her nuptials, but whose identity can never be revealed, after the bus suddenly set fire to itself on Causeway Head Road…

---

148 Mr Stacky O'Shea to give him his full name.

Of Dore

My song from the middle of France in the middle of a day in the middle of an August, stuck in the middle of the family diary, for Megan's fifth birthday in 1991.

This is not a broken leg
This is not an old beer keg
This is not an old shoe seg
This is just a song for Meg
For Meg of Dore
Isn't four
Any more.

Being four was formidable
Being five is finer
Now Meg isn't four no more
We'll have to wine and dine her
Being four's not the same as five
My Meg's joined the famous five…

Our Holiday
A story from the family diary, written on the old black and white Hercules computer 1992.

When I Went to Greece
by Aphra Thom

When I went to Greece we went on a bike ride.
We went on an aeroplane to Greece.
I sat next to Kate O' Shea.
When we had lunch I sat next to Rose O' Shea.
The sky was very blue and the sun was very yellow.
And we stayed in a house with a balcony with it.
We had a swim every day and my favourite food was sausages.

Our Holidays With The Dooberry
From the holiday diaries, *passim*

The stories of the *Dooberry* can only be safely told on holidays, out in the open, when the full gang is there, including Kate and Rosie and Tom O'Shea.

Usually, some kind of container has been washed up near where we are walking in Xante or Brittany or the Hope Valley or London.

Out of it comes a Dooberry.

The stories always feature two Alans.

One is Good Alan.

And one is Bad Alan.

They are identical except for a tattoo on Good Alan's left bottom cheek. Bad Alan sometimes puts a tattoo on his bottom cheek to mislead the storyteller. But he doesn't know his left from his right.[149]

---

149 Or indeed his bottom from his elbow, if he is the Alan O'Shea who was born under a table in a bungalow on Marples night, went to King Ted's and Oxford, became a teacher in London, lived in a teacher's commune, was driven mad by cultural studies and three children, and had no food at his wedding where I was the best man, but Jenny still married him anyway.
There is a Mr O'Shea in everything I write. He is often the caretaker.

Opon
From Eleanor's Word Book Y 3W, included in the family diary 1989.

Scremed
Thort
Carefully
Knock
Anserd
Opon
Agein
Crick
Hllo
Alin
Rokcit
Voycie
Because
Picher
Plece
Hores
France
Thorgho

Oh Dear, Nanny's Got Stuck in the Freezer!
A song from the family diaries 1991.

When Nanny got stuck in the freezer
We didn't know what to do
We didn't know whether to go for a wee
Or whether to go for a poo
We didn't know whether to ring the doctor
Or to ring the vet
When Nanny got stuck in the freezer
We think she's still there yet.

Pardon-moi!
from a holiday diary 1993.

After lunch at the back of the butchers at Dompierre Les Eglises, somewhere near Limoges, we are given champagne and asked to join in *Yellow Submarine* with some French diners. One of them, Yvette, kisses Rony and dances with him. A second woman half an hour later dances with him on a road near a lake. He celebrates with a song for the Autoharp.

The Song of The Trottoir

She kissed me on the trottoir
(You should have seen me)
She kissed me on the trottoir
(And I said oui oui)
She kissed me on the trottoir
There was not a lot our
Lot could do
When she kissed me on the trottoir
At quarter past two.

G C G A7 D7 G D7 G

*

Robinson's songs are undistinguished
Anthony Everett (Birmingham Post)

Pen friend
From a family diary 1993.

Could you tell me what is your own whole name?
Like (Megan Aphra Robinson Thom)
I live in a stone built house with my dad, Mum sister and brother.
Our pets are a fish, hamster and two cats.
The insterment's that I play are violin piano Irish whistle and recorder. What insterments do you play?
I am 8 year's of age how old are you?
I go to Dore Junior School. I would like to now what school you go to?
This is a picture of my family.

Piano Exams, Mr Firth's Trousers
And Pasta Tuna Bake
From the family diary 1994.

Megan has ducks in Mr Scholey's classroom, and some roller skates at home. Goronwy speaks some French, and goes to France. Someone goes to Eyam.

There are piano exams and a trip to the SY Festival at Wortley, where we see falcons. Our rabbit is taken by a fox.

On the County School bonfire night we see Mrs Holding, but it's not as good as when Mr Firth lit his trousers last year.

Eleanor gets grade 1 with 118 points.

Goronwy goes round Coronation Street and -

> *Tim Robinson creosoted the shed and talked about God.*

At Scarborough we see the Swinging Blue Jeans on the Spa, sail on the *Regal Lady* and stay at the *Villa Esplanade*. We also go to Almeria in Spain, swim nude, meet the Bagshaws and a drug dealer.

We play Cluedo.

The school adopts the slogan *Striving for Excellence*. We think it's silly.

We see Take That, ride on the first Supertram, and dance at the Thursday folk dancing at school. We bike round Derwent, and on a wet day in Wales see a demonstration of slate splitting.

We remember the *Acromaniacs,* go to Chatsworth, see *Dracula* in Oldham, play cafes at *Heart's* restaurant on the *conservatory table,* and at the Wheatsheaf in Baslow Steph[150] has pasta tuna bake -

> *Yum yum.*

---

150 Stephanie Lorna Robinson, who's held us all together for years. Geth's daughter, my only niece, and the sister I never had.

Princess Diana and Death Row
From the family diary 1997.

We swim at Hathersage, and play *Come on Meg!*

Goronwy's application for circus school describes him as -

> *The fourth best club juggler in Europe.*

He says he expects to spend his life performing and encouraging other people to perform.

Megan writes -

> *I don't feel exited at all which is really wired because the night before my birthday I usually do. This is my first decade finished. In 02 hours 48 minutes and 7 seconds I will be 11.*

Princess Diana dies the day we get back from Scarborough. Megan tells the tale of Mr Snig who is in love with a girl who looks like a post-box. We do games marathons. Viv wins.

*

Eleanor and Rony have a written dialogue on the settee at Brandon's piano lesson at 4.20 pm while Megan does her scales.

> **ELEANOR**
> Can I go and sleep over at Katie Dore on Friday and go and see *The Full Monty* with her then as well? Yes/no to staying over?
> **RONY**
> No.
> **ELEANOR**
> Yes/no to seeing *The Full Monty?*
> **RONY**
> Yes.
> **ELEANOR**
> Why no to staying over?
> **RONY**
> Because I love you and I like to be with you on Saturday mornings. And for other reasons too.
> **ELEANOR**
> You're just being selfish. And what other reasons?

RONY
The Alsatian might bite you.
ELEANOR
It won't.
RONY
Too much telly.
ELEANOR
No, that's the same at home.
RONY
Not enough nutritious food.
ELEANOR
Same at home.
RONY
You might mix up your Katie's.
ELEANOR
I don't think so.
RONY
Homework, piano, room, decorating.
ELEANOR
Done them all (not).
RONY
Other reasons.
ELEANOR
What?

*

Viv gets her new job in *Excess and Giddiness* at Hallam Uni.

Eleanor makes guacamole with 4-year-old prawns.

Megan writes -

> *Dear cleaners please do not dismantle any of my dens. This is by not moving the sofa taking my light down and not moving any cushions or the red checked rug very important please because it took me ages to build and I would get mad. Yours faithfully*

Stuck in the diary is a ticket to *Giselle* at the Lyceum, a programme for a sponsored walk, and a cutting about Helen Daniels dying in *Neighbours* - end of an era![151]

---

151 Nobody knew which one had died, Helen or Anne Haddy, till both had.

Viv takes Goronwy to Circus School in London and leaves him there, but he comes back and says -

> I wasn't aware of the difference between Dore and Hackney. 5 minutes down here you'll find a nice sports centre. 5 minutes down the road in Hackney you'll find a crack dealer.

*

There's a letter from Viv's parents about moving to the seaside, and the food they had at their goodbye party in Dorking.

There are notes from Lily about what we did in our holidays, and as always she spells *Goronwy* with only one o.

Megan writes -

> I feel awful, my throat hurts my ear just popped so all in all I feel absolutely shit & its not because I'm tired so don't say that. This happened a few days ago as well and I'm going hot then cold and I hate it so there and don't ask 'What do you want me to do about it?' because I don't know it just hurts - Love Megan

There are photos of Agas, and Megan's measurements of how many bacteria grew after 12 hours.[152]

*

And tucked into the big family diary is a diary from Greece, after a holiday with the O'Sheas, with lists everyone wrote while waiting for the plane home.

Best
…the swim at that deep blue and green sea or the taverna where we ate the old hen…doing the hokey kokey in the sea and driving in the Panda… pink ice cream… swimming in the waves at Petani and also eating crème caramel

Worst
It ended…being woken up by bulldozers knocking the house down…I like snorkelling, do not like pizza…the squeaky bed...the curly haired taxi driver…

---

152 16,777,216.

Lost

...the plastic disc for the baby bottle...sandals...spade...sleep...
necklace...patience...the drift of story of the Dooberry...

Nearly lost

...my snorkel...my HE Bates book

Found

...Goronwy...Viv's necklace...

Lost forever

...the buggy tyre...Kate's brace...the Sunday Times (good
riddance)... Goronwy snorkel...Alan's antique aqua sun hat

And there's an account of a very early morning story walk with Rosie O'Shea,
seeing a dead centipede, a black wolf, a square full of shadows, a band, a
church full of candles, and a bus station full of rusty old buses.

*

Eleanor submits her novel *Handcuffed to Death Row* for her English
homework, plus the favourable reviews that go with it, and her biog.

Writer Eleanor Thom age 14 lives in Totley with her parents, brother
and sister. She has two cats and is doing her grade 5 piano exams in
November. She has appeared in 2 plays and is currently rehearsing
for a play coming up in the autumn.

Peace and Roses
From the family diaries 1999

The Song of Fifteen Roses for Eleanor

Hey you say today's your birthday
Well have one tomorrow too
Anything you want you can
Anyone you want is you
I ain't too good at saying things
Don't mean I don't love you no
In the golden heart of your fifteenth winter
Let fifteen roses grow.

At every darkest daybreak
Deep in every field of snow
In the ironed heart of winter
Fifteen roses grow.

Poem Night

Once upon a late teatime, when the kids weren't quite in bed, but should have been, I sat down to type as many kids' poems as I could type at one go, for this John Foster bloke who had been on *Cherwell* years before, and was now about to launch this prestige kids' poetry series for the Oxford University Press.

He'd just rung and asked me to pop anything I'd got in the post. At £75 a pop. For tomorrow.

I hadn't anything to pop so I said I had, and then sat down to pop some.

First I wrote some acrostic birthday cards.

Then some Bobdylannny and Dylanthomassy pieces.

Then, warming up, a family tree poem in the shape of a family tree, some ballads, a few sheets of free verse, and then some imprisoned verse.

Then Welsh and French, concrete, Japanese and Chinese verse. Then limericks, haikus, villanelles, couplets, thriplets, sestinas, rhymed, rhythmed, unrhymed and unrhythmed, in-and-out-the-dusky-bluebelly poems and -

I didn't stop until twenty minutes before the last post at the GPO in town, twenty-two minutes away by fast car.

Loads of the poems were published over the next few years in Foster's and other books, then cannibalised into other people's books, and literacy hours, syllabuses, model lessons, school assembly source books, and English as a second and third language courses all over the world. A few poetic cheques still arrive, and classfuls of kids still suddenly write, saying thanks, with pictures and poems of their own.

We've Got a Wah Wah, coming next, is my most anthologised.

It's my only writing that will outlive me.

Frighten the child in your life by reading it to them and send a small poetic cheque to the Children's Hospital, and say it's from me?

Queer Claws

We've got a Wah Wah at our house
Squelchy as an octopus and scratchy as a mouse
Slippy and slurpy
Ever so dirty
And slimy
Cor blimey
Nose all runny
Cheeks all funny
Claws all queer
And its tail-oh dear
We've got a Wah Wah comes at night!
Waits in my bedroom to give my Dad a fright!

We've got a Wah Wah only I can see
Comes out at night but just for me
Nasty and knobbly
Wibbly and wobbly
Swishy and slow
And its teeth oh no!
Lips all lumpy
Bum all bumpy
We've got a Wah Wah come and see!
Something something something very nice to me!

I'm going to take my Wah Wah to school
Even if it's against the rule
Bubbly and squelchy something and belchy
Doesn't wash
And it's something oh gosh
Feet all soppy
Something sloppy
I've got a Wah Wah
Pleased to meet you
If you are nasty
My Wah Wah'll EAT YOU! [153]

---

153 Transcribed as closely as possible from the Internet from a performance by a class of kids at Munford Primary School, wherever that is. I've no hard copies of Wah Wah left and it's long freed into the oral tradition. Wah!

Rare Feat

I'd written loads about family crack-ups, long before I even had a family to crack.

Therapists might be interested.[154]

In *Frankly Frankie*, which I started in 1980 and which still knocks around in some schools, Frankie has come north with Mum and five-month-old Tina, but Dad's stayed in London. Mum's drinking. The new school is horrid and the kids all have blocked northern noses.

> *Here Frankie the principal sufferer from a matrimonial disaster lets us understand his/her thoughts about what has occurred. The heart-warming play is given extra interest because the part of Frankie can be read or acted equally convincingly by a boy or a girl. Rony Robinson has achieved in this play a rare feat of dramatic invention.*
> The editor of the Macmillan edition of Frankly Frankie

This rare feat of dramatic invention ends -

MOGSIE
Is that the end then Frankie?
FRANKIE
Things don't end do they? Not like in books and plays. You're happy. Or unhappy. And then you have to carry on till you're not.
MOGSIE
It looks like the end of me. There's only one more speech.
FRANKIE
Oh yes.

*

In *I Want Doesn't Get* (Faber 1990) the sassy mother bolts on the first page, and ten-year-old Julian tells the story of life without her, with bravery, footnotes and a dog.

> *A funny, serious, crazy book*
> Naomi Lewis (Observer)

*

---

154 They weren't.

BT used to run a biennial festival in which amateur theatre groups could get scripts of a new play by a real playwright, to perform without paying royalties for one week only, with free posters and t-shirts.

I was one of their real playwrights for 1999, and my *No Love Lost* had 47 simultaneous world premieres all over the UK, including the one I directed at the Lantern Theatre in Nether Edge, with my Eleanor as the deserted daughter who stops talking because of her parents' selfishnesses. Her Dad[155] is Max Johnson[156] a history teacher who's just retired on his 60th birthday, and the play starts with his surprise party. He tells his story backwards until the interval, when his wife Kate, who is a good amateur actor, leaves him, and, in Act Two tells her version of what happened next, going forwards.

It's fun and confusing - and fun and confusing to write too, needing graphs and 3D diagrams. Samuel French published it, and it still gets performed in unexpected places with unexpected casts. There was a black version in Tottenham, a bucolic one in Bawtry, and a few years ago the TOADS brought it all back home to Totley.

Just before the end, the split couple are alone at last -

> **KATE**
> What's next Max?
> **MAX**
> I'm a historian. I only know things when they've happened and don't matter any more. What about you?
> **KATE**
> I'm an actor. Someone has to prompt me.
>
> *This could be their moment, say the stage directions, but the door bursts open.*

---

155 In the play.
156 !

The Best Advice Jenny O' Shea Ever Gave Anyone About Bringing Up Kids And What To Do When It All Gets Too Hard And You Don't Feel You Are Up To The Job
from a Holiday Diary c 1994.

It never stays as bad as it's got… and it never stays as good either.

9. Eric Shaw Was In The Cremorne

Radio Sheffield Changed My Life! (Again)
or
The Naked Broadcaster

I'd come back to live full-time in Sheffield in 1981.

Dave Sheasby asked me to script and read and record a weekly column, a sort of *Letter From Totley,* for Radio Sheffield's education programme broadcast on Fridays afternoons, while the rest of the BBC were in the *Broomhill Tavern,* meeting the public.

Nine months later the BBC asked me to be a presenter of programmes, unscripted and live. I've done it happily ever after.

*

Joining the BBC was like starting school again, when the older kids are all glamorous and larger-than-life, with funny names, and it's all a bit magic really.

Radio Sheffield was magic. How could there even be radio programmes broadcast from a house in Broomhill?

And the BBC people were larger-than-life, even when they were actually very small, like most of the actual Capsticks and Cookes actually were when you met them on the other side of your wireless.

They did have funny names too. There were two Peter Harrisons, several other Peters and at least three Coopers, plus Bill and Don the gardening men who didn't always even know which one they were. There were Tims galore, and character-shifting women whose names wouldn't stay still *(Dinah? Diane? Dianna?)* The poshest sounding - and they all sounded posh, even when they went on to do trademark Yorkshire after - was Alison Allen-Booth, who got up early on Fridays to go to Sheaf market to price up cabbages. The education producer, with his economics degree from the LSE, doubled up as *Captain Westbourne* the racing tipster. There were impossible, beautiful women in the office, and at Christmas they all set fire to themselves in Paradise Square.

In those days listeners rang up to tell everyone whenever they'd got stuck behind their wardrobes. You could swap your old fridge for some used bedding, live on air. There were competitions when you had to identify phone boxes.

*

174

But 60 Westbourne Road itself wasn't always the glamorous home of the glamorous BBC.

It was a glamorous spy centre in the days of the Marples, especially down in its cellars. Before that, and before the blitz blitzed half of it, it was a glamorous mansion, with its own Ballroom and Italian gardens, tall marble fireplaces and deep windows, all surrounded by the prep schools, botanical gardens, and all the raffish fun of Broomhill. Half the house was sealed off but you could still see it through one glass-panelled upstairs door, unpainted since 1936.

I could never work out at Westbourne Road which room we were in, up and down the dusty staircases, and in and out of the CS Lewis doors.

It was like being in a weekly rep, all dodge and swerve, with the constant possibility of the police or the bailiffs dropping in, or of postmen arriving with paternity orders. An escape via the fireplace was always imminent. The performers were stuck at the limit of their talent, loved by their audiences just for being there in this forgotten provincial town, but still hoping to be whisked away to London by an agent or a lover at the end of the season.

But meanwhile they held tight, and didn't bump into the furniture much. They went on Ealing Comedy strikes. One of their own bosses sued them for libel, just because they'd all signed a letter saying he was useless.[157]

*

The week I signed on for my first solo broadcast, the *Dramatis Personae,* according to the *Radio Times* were -

> Gordon Harrison
> John Fleet
> Roger Moffat
> Robert Jackson (sport and local galas)
> Nigel Hallam on Sunday
> Dinah Maiden and Winton Cooper for breakfast
> Tony Capstick
> Jack Baker
> Michael Cooke
> Bob Hazelwood
> Dave Brennan
> Mel Hague,
> Pat Sleath Sean Kennedy and Link.
> Vincent Bradley

*

---

157 As if!

Seconds after I'd signed off from my first show, Frank Mansfield, who'd got me there in the first place, came in to give me, to keep for ever, two 12" reel-to-reel tapes recording it. He had written on the box -

A star is born!

The Manager asked me up to his office to drink whisky. Goronwy joined me and drank orange till he was sick all over the Manager's trousers.

I drank three quarters of the whisky, but it had no effect.[158]

Strong stuff, radio.

---

158 But I mislaid the reel-to-reel historic tapes for ever.

Rony's Friends The Stars

So?

Wanna know about my friends the stars?

Some of the famous people and celebs I've met through my lifetime's service to broadcasting and the arts?

*

Which famous people have you met? is a favourite phone-in topic, right up there with -

> *Should you let your dog sleep with you?*

And -

> *Hanging, how would you like it?*

And -

> *Dog dirt - like or lump it?*

When we do famous people someone's always recently spotted John Prescott on Doncaster Station. Someone else has often been behind Susan Maugham at Lidl. And seen Elvis in the sauna at Ponds Forge. And Lord Adonis with the Duke of Darnall in the Rising Sun at Fulwood. And David Blunkett driving round Shiregreen in his Lagonda.

*

Some people ask -

> *Actually, I bet you've met loads of interesting celebrities and stars and famous people?*

What they actually mean is -

> *Actually, aren't you lucky to meet all those interesting celebrities and stars and famous people, with you being such a nobody?*

Well actually, celebrities and stars and famous people aren't very interesting at all. They're always selling something, or they'd not be seen dead on the radio with you. And they're usually not on the radio with you anyway, but miles away in some London studio, being interviewed down ISDN lines by local radio DJs, at seven minute intervals, all day, being asked the same questions they've themselves suggested, and never the ones that should be asked.[159]

*

Still want to know about some of my friends the stars?

Famous people and celebs I've met?

OK.

Joan Baez, then
Django Bates
JP Bean
Dave Berry [160]
Eric Bibb, Eric Webb of Cantley
Bishop Jack, Bishop John, and Harold Bishop (in the balcony at Buxton Opera House)
Blair, who was very sweaty both times
Brenda Blethyn, who told my daughters in Manchester that she had had a crush on me in Coventry[161]
Boycott (I'll boycott him next time)
&
David Bradley, Dai Bradley, Hedley Salt and at least one member of the Hedley Ward Trio
Melvyn Bragg and Billy Bragg
Dave Brennan
Marti Caine (and Frank Abel)
Jimmy Carol, Carol Robson
Chas and Dave, Sue and Dave, Dave and Sue
Joe Cocker, Vic Cocker
Peter Cooper, Robert Cooper who did the amazing radio Beano, Lucy Crapper, Patrick Crapper and Peter Cropper
Michael Cooke, and that little ready steady cook
&
George Cunningham in a pickle, Edwina Currie, Edwina Currie's Spitting

---

159 E.g. How much are you getting?
160 We've done a gig together at the National Centre For Popular Music (the one that wasn't very popular) and nobody came. The £100 cheques bounced. Frank White was diddled too.
161 Now she tells me...

178

Image puppet, the Corrie girl from High Storrs, Tony Currie, Lyn Perry from Corrie, and Lynne Perry from Sacramento whose mother encouraged me with the Autoharp, and maybe shouldn't have
&
Jenny Day (and Angela Knight)
The Dowager Duchess of Devonshire, (and John Cornwell) Max Nottingham of Lincoln, (and Bruce Kent)(and Jenny Derbyshire)[162]
Derek Dooley, Sean Dooley.
Candida Doyle, Rex Doyle
Jeff Ennis Jess Ennis
John Foster the baker,[163] John Foster the anthologiser
Peter Fox, Edward Fox, Sam Fox and Sharon from Foxhill
Martin Gordon, Daniel Gordon (and Clarrie Jordan and Jordan Gould)
Bomber Graham, Graham and Stuart from Tesco
Michael Gough and Goff the estate agent
Harry Gration, Jimmy Hagan
Bob, Hilary and Page Hall
Ken Hawley and Richard Hawley
Stephanie Hazeldine[164] of course
Ray Hearne from the Dearne
Matt Helders the monkey and his mum
David Heslop the oxymoron
George Hill the folkie, Alan Hill the bookie, Howard Hill, Howard Holmes the anti-racist, Melanie Hill, Snig Hill where I've broadcast from
&
Billy Hukin, Pukin' Hukin
Derek Jacobi who's been Bottom, and Dr Jacobs at the Limes Grove Practice who's seen my bottom
Barry Jackson, Helen Jackson, Robert Jackson, Stuart Jackson
Max Jaffa squeezed and John Kirkpatrick squeezing
Marina Lewitzka on her tractor
Jack Laden in his wardrobe, Lady Garden in the Peace Gardens,
Joan Littlewood, Pie Face Littlewood
Vic Martin's Jimmy Martin
Alistair McGowan before he was whoever he is now, in Ipswich, and Ian McMillan before he was, too, in Barry Hines's kitchen
&
Stanley Matthews, who I played football with, and Kaliq Meer
Two murderers in Lindholme and one man in Bakewell who spent 27 years in

---

162 And David Essex, who'd dyed.
163 We don't want a bigger slice of the cake: we want the bloody bakery! - Red Ladder badge
164 It's double heading when two radio presenters do a show together. Steph and Jenny Day are my doubleheaded best, and I loved them as much as listeners did. (But that Paulette Edward's and me…)

prison for a murder he didn't do
Ruby Murray
Johnny Nelson
Michael Palin of this parish and Matthew Parris who wouldn't quite come out
with it
Fred Pass, Simon Pass
Katie Patmore who likes dogs
Suzanne Phillips, Trevor Phillips's brother
Peter Price (but not Katie Price), Frank Prince, Prince Naz (but not Prince)
Nick Robinson, and the other Nick Robinson
Jane Rogers and Roy Rogers (but not that one)
Ian Rotherham and Emma Barnsley, both from Sheffield and Matthew
Dronfield from Brightside Lane and the Dronfield Handbell Ringers who
somehow ring a bell & Sheila Rowbotham (and Margaret Bottom and Annie
Bottomley)
Joe Scarborough (and Rod Hull)(unless it was Bernie Clifton)
Kid Shillitoe, Alan Sillitoe, and a nephew of Percy Sillitoe
Denis Skinner, David Skinner, Dave Skinner as was
Helen Shapiro, Sid Kipper, Sid of Waterthorpe, two Sitwells, Skippy o' Totley
Eric Smith, Kevan Smith, Linda Smith
David Steel, Tommy Steele, Tom Steel, Steeleye Span's Maddy Prior (and a
distant relation of Iron Hague's)
Nikki Stoddart of United Agents
Doris Stokes, and the other Doris who both forgot to come back on the radio
after they were dead like they said they would, and Doris Askham
Ian Soutar and John Tams (funny names funny people)
Mary and Neil Warnock
Billie and Willie Whitelaw
Anne Widdicombe and Professor Widdowson
Don and Shirley Williams
&
Terry Wogan, who thought he was so funny
An X Factor winner whose name I've so lost
Paula Yates who was so rude
And Madame Zucchini who is funny and rude with vegetables

*

Oh, and talking about famous people, once upon a really long ago time
on Deptford High Street, I was pushing Goronwy in his buggy back from
Deptford Green Comprehensive school. I was doing a term there as resident
writer (though the kids weren't very resident) and heading back to our
Deptford council flat already dreaming I was asleep.

And there she was. And it was her, even if she didn't look quite right because famous people never do. They try too hard, and they are always smaller than they should be.

She was in the back of this really big shiny black car.

Now, Deptford High Street's a bit rough even in daylight, but there's a pretty old church just beyond the bridge and it's called St Paul's, and is really popular for funerals, except when it's raining, because the lead roof's usually been pinched.

So it wasn't that unusual for a big shiny black car to be sliding down the High Street with Mum in flowers on the roof and poor old Mum in her coffin in the back

The trouble was, that this poor old Mum wasn't in her coffin at all.

She was three feet from us, on her own, propped against the back window. Smaller than she should have been. Wearing glasses, which she didn't, then. With her eyes open. Looking. At us. As if she knew us.

And then, and this is when it happened, and it was just like when you see people you've seen on the telly, she mouthed hello and waved, thinking she knew us.

We waved back, like you do. The lights changed and I said to Goronwy -

   That's the Queen!

No one's believed us. But it's true. She recognised us first.

So we were more famous than she was that day in Deptford.

Sheffield's Most Famous Son

The Opt-In Youth Theatre Company represented Sheffield in 2000 by performing my show *Charley* in the *Ronald McDonald* theatre at the Millennium Dome. Kids from all over Britain were going there a day-at-a-time all year to celebrate where they lived, and get a free burger.

Some VIP Sheffielders weren't pleased that I was the one writing our contribution, or that we had decided to celebrate 2000 glorious years of Sheffield with a play about a murderer.

But Charlie Peace - for it is he - is probably the most famous person who ever came from round here.

And apart from being a murderer, and a thief, he was also rather fun.

And very theatrical. He was escapologist, violinist, actor, inventor, magician, master of disguises, and maybe even a sort of Robin Hood.

And he was a storyteller too - so when he burgled Charles Dickens down in Peckham and caught him in bed with his mistress, he made him sit up and listen to his full life, including the lion, and our Charlie would have ended up in *Edwin Drood* if the other Charlie hadn't dropped down dead first.

Or maybe I made that up.

Anyway, we took our Charlie Peace to London in *Charley* to celebrate the life and death of an ordinary Sheffielder who wasn't ordinary any more than any of us are, though most of us stay hidden from history.

He isn't hidden. Because he was a murderer and a fugitive, we know loads about him. We know the poverty of his childhood with a crippled father, after his industrial injury with the lion. We know about the industrial injury Charlie sustained on his 14th birthday in the steel works. We know about his years as a hopeless theatrical, burglar and adulterer who then became his own myth for just two years, a pimpernel, and a rich successful inventor and organiser of musical soirees, a man of advanced opinions who wrote progressive letters to the press about Empire and prison reform. And humanitarian scaffolds. A man who blacked up with burnt cork so no one would find him but when they did, dived from the train taking him home, at 40 mph, still handcuffed to a twenty stone copper, while twenty thousand Sheffielders waited on the station to welcome him back.

His life makes you ask - made him ask - questions.

In Sheffield he met Edward Carpenter and the socialists up Scotland Street (or maybe I made that up too). But the question still remains - in a city of such inequality, who are the real burglars?

And how can the rich ever be rich without robbing the poor?

Our Millennium Dome play *Charley* was a twenty-minute verse play for a cast of fifty, with real historic film, jogalong verse and samba. It got performed again a month later at the *Crucible*, preceded this time by the world premiere of a documentary play telling the story of us doing the show in London, where we suffered cackly cockneys, itchy cozzies, and rank hair. And where Jack went missing and Big Ben got the time wrong because of the pigeons.

> *Charley came to London*
> *Just like we have done*
> *Even came to Greenwich*
> *Thought he'd join the fun*

The VIPs who came with us to Greenwich weren't impressed. Nor were *McDonalds*. But I was. Especially by the kids, as always, and by the Chris who directed them.

> *You can be like Charley*
> *You can dare to dream*
> *You can make a world up*
> *Where nothing's what it seems.*

Talking To Women In Bed

Rony Robinson has probably talked to more women in bed on a Saturday morning than any other man in Sheffield.
The Star

Tony &

Tony Capstick should have played Charlie Peace in a show of course.[165]

The show he and I actually did was *Tony and Rony* on the BBC.

He did the first hour from 9, and then we did two hours together.

When everyone switched off, it was just me.

I'd asked to work from separate studios, so I could concentrate on preparing my own ad-libs, and try not to smoke. I also asked to *drive the desk* for my two hours because, on radio, whoever drives the desk drives the show. Unjealous and unargumentative as Tony was, and he was, he was a bugger when he had control, talking till he accidentally said something funny, then crashing in the music.

He could have resented me crashing in on him of course.

But he didn't.

He said nice things about me even when I wasn't there. And because everyone loved him, some of them eventually loved me too. People still come up and talk about *Tony and Rony,* and how good he is on it.

*

Funny chap. The funniest.

He told his own life and adventures so well you didn't mind that he didn't listen much to yours.

He was a friend of the police but he kept getting into trouble with them.

He was a folk-singing lefty who was fascinated by the army and guns.

He never paid for any of the *masho* tea he always talked about on the radio, but he paid for booze for anybody.

He was more interested in sex than anyone I've ever known, even me.

I never saw him angry but there was something in him that was.

---

165 Of chuffing course!

I've tried to write him into stories and plays, but never got near. Perhaps people didn't.

I'd like to have spoken at his funeral, but at least I managed to write about him in the *Telegraph,* and include the tale of him kissing me outside the *Frog and Parrot* on Division Street, when we had both been drinking for charity.

The kissing went down badly with the Capstick supporters, but my big break-up with them was a year later, when I was doing a live phone-in about the BBC, and a Capstick fan rang in to ask why they'd sacked their best broadcaster?

I said yes, Tony was the best broadcaster. But he drank too much. And really it was surprising he'd not been sacked earlier.

Well I drink too much myself, so I wasn't being holy. For years boozing hadn't affected his work, and even when it had, he was still better than any of us until, say, the last year.

The Capstick supporters made accusations, but I don't think (this time) there was any boss's conspiracy, e.g. to give Tony an impossible slot in the mornings so he would fail, so he could be sacked, so he'd die.

I said so on air.

The papers took up the story, and were nastier than I expected. The family complained.[166] I haven't met any of them since, or been invited to any of their gigs.

But I still mention Tony whenever possible. I can't walk past the *Frog and Parrot* without remembering him.

Or Grindleford Station.

*

---

166 Tony and Rony- the Adjudication
BBC Radio Sheffield 29 January 2004
Mrs Capstick complained the presenter of this phone-in programme unfairly blamed drinking problems for her late husband's dismissal by the radio station. She also complained discussion of the topic on air infringed Mr and Mrs Capstick's privacy without justification. Ofcom decided that it was not unfair for the presenter to respond to a caller criticism by explaining the true reasons for Mr Capstick's dismissal. As these reasons are in the public domain the discussion did not infringe Mr or Mrs Capstick's privacy.
The Ofcom Executive Fairness Group.

My best Capstick was in an empty, rainy tent at the Abbeydale Industrial
Hamlet years ago, singing to his guitar, to himself -

> *To be a Sheffield grinder it is no easy trade*
> *There's more than you'd imagine to the grinding of a blade*
> *The strongest man among us is old at thirty two*
> *There's few who brave such hardships as we poor grinders do.*

Tonight at the Crucible, a Comedy in 5 Acts

Act 1
1972
I write the second-ever play in the Studio, *Edward Carpenter Lives!* It transfers to the Main House. I write *Lunch Duty,* which is performed in the Studio at lunchtimes.[167]

Act 2
1973
I write *Free For All,* a second play about Edward Carpenter, and am appointed Resident Writer under Colin George. I write a kid's show, and a play in three weeks. I direct *Graft* and the management collapses. Colin goes to Hong Kong. I am sent to Coventry.

Act 3
1976
Living in exile, I write freelance for the *Crucible* including *One Day in Sheffield.* I co-write *Jokers 1 and 2* and end up as Resident Writer with Clare Venables at *The Theatre Royal Stratford East* just as she and her management collapse.

Act 4
1981
Returned home, I am appointed Resident Writer at the *Crucible* (again) under Clare Venables who coincidentally now has the top job there. I write *Child's Play,* which she directs, and is a triumph, and *See You Next Tuesday,* which isn't quite. She quarrels with me and I never know why. I go into exile again, after *Jokers 3.* Her management collapses.

Act 5
1996
Under the new artistic director I am recalled to improve *Stirrings* (and don't). I write *United on a Wednesday Night,* a community play of two halves that ended with a derby football match on the grass there used to be between the theatres. And then, under the new new artistic director, *A Naughty Night To Swim In* about going mad.

Posh men take over the *Crucible* and I head for the bar.[168]

---

167 'Magnificent Maggie McCarthy,' says the Stage. She is. And so's Maire her events-organising sister who does the amazing Chance to Dance on the hot streets of Sheffield every year. I rented a house Maire had had in Coventry once, and a generation later my Eleanor acted with her Charlotte. I also include her, and her, here now, on the Green Un principle of mentioning as many names as poss, so they all have to buy a copy. For charity remember?
168 The bar has moved and everything seems smaller now, like your pasts are supposed to.

Terminal

I Killed My Mother: Live Radio Show Told

- was the headline over the front-page story of the Yorkshire Post on December 2nd 2000.

> *Stunned radio listeners heard a heartbroken man sob as he confessed on a live phone-in show to killing his terminally-ill mother.*

The police came round within the hour, and they investigated for ages. John of Dronfield was the heartbroken man, though I'm not sure he'd either *confessed or sobbed.* But he did have nine months of hassle. His four-year-dead mother was dug up again. He was finally let off with the severest bollocking.

He took me out for a drink after.

The moral might be don't admit things on the radio - people might be listening.

But I think John was brave (he insisted on using his own name) and helped his cause, at a huge cost.

I wasn't brave. Or very quick. John's phone number was scribbled in the Programme Diary, and was the only way he could ever have been found. If I had guessed what was coming, or been a better journalist, I could have lost that diary before the police came and demanded it.

Tons Of Things I Wouldn't Have Done Without Radio Chuff[169]

I walk onto the pitch at Bramall Lane in front of a capacity crowd and give the match-ball to the ref, with 15,000 Blades watching.[170] I have my United kit on underneath my suit, in case they need me.

I speak to the Old Edwardian's Dinner where old boys gather to thank God they didn't go to schools with the working class or girls. I tell them what I think of their King Edward's. What I think is, it was pigshit.

Twice I go to the baths in the centre of Doncaster where the Beatles once played. Twice I go below, and remove my clothes and broadcast live and naked from the lemon steam room and the 1930's sauna full of deckchairs and jockeys. On each occasion my beautiful assistants stay clothed and red. I appear in the *News Of The World,* as one day I knew I would –

> *Sheffield presenter Rony Robinson stripped naked to broadcast from Turkish bath in Doncaster, Yorks.*

I climb a gasometer at Neepsend, as it moves.

I walk round summer Page Hall with Nikki Hibberd in her spiked floral hair, and rejoice that, when the Council erected a planter to celebrate *Page Hall in Bloom,* not only were the flowers not pinched, but the people of Page Hall planted extra ones.

Capstick and I introduce a Christmas Philharmonic concert at a packed City Hall. I tell the story of the two things that used to happen at All Saints School at the Christmas parties where everyone brought stuff and pooled. One was that everyone wanted to eat everyone else's mother's food. The other was that (cf. the feeding of the five thousand) there was always stuff left over. So there are still miracles! Co-operation and sharing! Three thousand people clap like it's Christmas.

I sit for three hours in the *Women Against Pit Closures* caravan outside Markham Main, where no men ever sit. I enter the Women's Cultural Club down the little alley between the Showroom and the café, on *Grinders Hill.* I am the only man who having got in, gets out.

---

169 I think calling it Radio Chuff was the invention of the Reiki chuckler Jen Coldwell, when she was press officer at the Crucible. She told me years later that she called the other one Radio Halitosis
170 Eric Shaw, uber Blades fan and my nephew-in-law, was in the Cremorne and missed it.

I fly in a hot-air balloon over Nottinghamshire and Jenny Day sits on me as we crash in a stubbly cornfield.

I am in a swinger's club in Attercliffe, with my recording machine and Stephanie Barnard my BBC producer. When the recording is done, we are shown two further cubicles where they do things I'd never thought of before (but often think of now).

I stand at Spurn Point at dawn, eating a bacon sandwich, waiting for a boat to carry me through the galloping waves to the warship waiting for me out there.

I am in the downstairs loo at Radio Sheffield. The nurse tells me to remove my trousers. We check me for testicular cancer, live on air.

I voice-over the film of the Sheffield Flood. When my second-niece Caitlin is shown it at her school, she tells everyone *Rony's her uncle.* They don't believe her.

Joan Baez gives me a signed CD. Joe Cocker tells me he's given up drinking. I'm disappointed. I tell him I know his brother. Peggy Seeger offers to tune my Autoharp after breakfast.

I march with the Miners on the day they go back after the Great Strike, and pretend I am one.

I fly with a listener in a four-seater plane over Totley.

I go to the fertility clinic at the Hallamshire. I start recording. I am counselled. I am given a plastic cup and shown the hatch outside. I am led into a small room with a chair, a small coffee table with a drawer, some tissues and a bowl of flowers. The door is shut. I am still recording. I open the drawer in the small coffee table and check on the magazines there. With the tape still running, I become a sperm donor.

I sit on a sofa interviewing William Whitelaw and the Earl of Scarborough, at the Earl's pad. His pedigree dogs wee on the Radio Sheffield boss who is sitting on the floor sucking up to them, and trying to get his tape recorder to work.

It is the night of the Millennium. Only one man in Yorkshire is sober. I am he. I am on the Town Hall balcony. At 43 seconds to the midnight of all our lives, Pauline Eveleigh checks the computerised electronic radio clock that has been purchased specially, because the Town Hall clock hasn't told the right time since 1897. Lord Mayors, Master Cutlers and Bishops flank me.

The electronic radio clock suddenly begins to race backwards. Fifteen thousand fellow citizens join in as I (inaccurately) count down to the new Millennium, and wait for the computers to crash and planes to drop out of the sky and the world to end, in which case mine will be the last voice ever heard in Sheff-

Tony in the Dark

So anyway, Tony and his mate have been rambling in Derbyshire.

They're 14.

They get back to Grindleford station.

Two posh schoolgirls are on the platform.

> *Yours looks a bit scruffy Angela!*

> *Good!*

Train comes in, all steamy.

Hasn't got a corridor.

> *Make sure you get off at the stop before the terminus Angela!*

> *Deidre!*

Girls get in empty compartment.

Watercolours of Sidmouth and Durham Cathedral.

Luggage racks. Bench seats. Leather window straps.

> *Take the kettle off before it boils Angela!*

> *Deidre!*

Guard calls to Tony and mate, still on the platform.

> *I think you could be in there, lads!*

> *Thanks mester!*

Tony and his mate open door.

> *Get your tickets punched there lads?*

> *Gee o'er mester!*

Girls cross-legged opposite sides, opposite ends.

Angela asks Tony his name. He tells her, when he remembers.

> *I like skiffle.*

> *I bet you do Tony.*

The other girl says -

> *As soon as this train departs for Sheffield it enters the second longest tunnel in England and there are seven minutes of dark thereafter.*

> *So?*

The Guard unfurls his flag.

The other girl says -

> *I notice you've got your little torches ready in your pockets boys? Or are you just pleased to see us?*

> *Deidre!*

Suddenly onto the platform, through the gushing steam, stagger two women ramblers.

Angela tells Tony what might happen.

Tony can't hear in all the rushing and gushing.

> *He's gone deaf!*

> *We know why don't we Deidre?*

Angela makes a whispered offer to Tony that no one has ever whispered to him before.

The women ramblers waddle for the train.

The guard blows his whistle.

The earth begins to move under Tony.

The train chuffs.

The guard ejaculates.

The - [171]

---

[171] The story Tony did risk finishing, when goaded, was about the patient at the Hallamshire who woke up on his trolley after the operation to hear the doctor saying, 'But nurse I said remove his spectacles!' His favourite story, though, was about the graveyard.

Tony In The Graveyard

This man's wife dies and she is very religious so he goes to this ornamental stonemason and orders her a gravestone to read -

She Were Thine!

The stonemason says -

Reet pal, it'll be up o'er her grave by next Sunday morning, I'll see thee reet. Reet?

So the widower goes away, and comes back next Sunday morning. There is a crowd round his wife's grave and they are laughing and pointing. He goes up to them and says -

What you lot reckon you're laughing and pointing at, then?

And they laugh and point at the gravestone, which says -

She Were Thin!

So the widower goes straight round to the monumental mason and says -

My wife was very religious. I asked you to provide a gravestone to show that, but when I got there everyone were laughing and pointing? You've missed off the 'e'!

And the ornamental mason pales and says -

I'll not charge thee. It's shocking that. I'll have it done reet for thee for next Sunday morning, so don't tha werrit!

So the widower goes away, and on the next Sunday morning he comes back to the churchyard and there is an even bigger crowd, laughing and pointing. He pushes through, and says -

What you lot reckon you're laughing and pointing at now? This is my dead wife's grave and she were very religious.

All they can do is point at the gravestone.

For it now says -

Eee She Were Thin!

The Five Shows That Changed Our Lives (Because Of What Happened After Them)

Peterloo (Sedgehill School SE6 1973)
Someone else's school play with long speeches I ended up producing, with red spotlights to wash the prostrate fifth year touching each other up while pretending to be the slain worker-heroes of 1819, with beer on empty stomachs to follow. A first night on a last night, and the beginnings of a dynasty.

Swamp Circus (Totley County School 1987)
Two circus performers in the corner of the playground, one ordinary afternoon, tempting anyone with any juggling balls to run away and join them. My Goronwy does, at 15.[172]

The Mysteries (National Theatre 1997)
Second time round, with Sue Johnston's Mary bursting out of her coffin, and my Megan getting kidnapped and taken off to Purgatory. Then, after, meeting Sue in the Green Room - we had been Belgrade pals – and thus my Eleanor getting her school work-experience on the third series of *The Royle Family*. Taken seriously, she becomes a comedian herself.[173]

Romeo and Juliet in The Dore Gang Show (Dore Village Hall 1998)
My Megan as Capulet[174] in my shrunk Shakespeare among the transvestite scoutmasters. Next stop singing with *Dead Like Harry* the Sheffield indie band, in dry ice at the packed City Hall. [175]

Alice (Harrogate Theatre 2001)
Alice is the theatre ghost, played by Shelley in my *Alice* directed by Rob Swain and getting four stars in the Guardian. My goodbye to theatre, my *Tempest,* and my story of a hundred years of pretending. The first new play

---

172 We were there the day he fell off the six-foot unicycle in Covent Garden at 18, and broke his arm, but he still finished the show even as the crowd were walking away. (How could they?) I was also there when he turned the audience round on a wet night in a club in Huddersfield, thank God, or we'd still both be there.

173 Especially as Bev in leopard skin and blonde wig. I didn't recognise her back stage on her first performance in Manchester. It was Bev and Co the Manchester Comedy Store had to delay the show for, by an hour, because the crowds were still winding right round the building demanding tickets.

174 Tybalt Prince of Cats, Megan corrects.

175 Then Rose Bruford Theatre School, and her wondrous Rose of Sharon there, and then all the rosy world's stages.

in living memory at Harrogate, it started by replaying the last five minutes of the previous show, and got more post-modern from then on. I didn't always understand it, but it was a triumphant first night. Also a last night and another ghost.

10. With Or Without Glasses

The Greek, The Dead Body And The Little Boy
or
How Radio Sheffield Changed My Life (Again)[176]

In 2001 I interviewed this arty woman about a village hall touring show she was going to do about rambling.

I saw her a few weeks later in a supermarket with a tall young man.[177]

I asked how her rambling show had gone.

She said it hadn't gone, didn't I listen to my own interviews? I could still come to its opening afternoon, at Wharncliffe Side, if I wanted?

I said in that case she could still come to my own not-yet-started night of new plays and sketches at the Lantern in Nether Edge, where I was about to give them my dead patient, my elderly Greek tourist with a 19-year-old wife, and my neglected 10-year-old who couldn't remember his lines even though he'd written them. She said she'd come. She did. We went to *The Stag* after.

She became Sally Goldsmith.[178]

---

176 The alphabetical order's gone to pieces. But why not? When did things ever happen in alphabetical order?

177 He turned out to be Ewan Townhead, named after the hippy abolish-money Lifespan commune at Townhead near Penistone where he was born. Guitarist, drummer, thinker, autodidact, supermarket stacker, dutchman, still tall, still a pal and still Sally's son.

178 The original Radio Sheffield interview that got me into the theatre, and the Letters from Totley recordings that got me into radio, and the interview with Sally the rambler, now my partner, all happened in what used to be the Ballroom at 60 Westbourne Road, however it changed over 30 years, in exactly the same place.

Tempuss, Ticker, Chandler & Co

Dinah
Our half Siamese more-white-than-black inherited cat that tore down the garden at 132 on the afternoon we moved in, raced to the top of the house, and stayed. She stays now, after we've gone, just beyond the leaning rose arch, and the pond, next to the hedge, near the orchard, just before the goosegogs, to the right of the acer on the left.

Ticker
The tortoise cat, rescued from Bradfield by Goronwy on the day we met my old Economics teacher, Mr Robinson, whose nickname had been Ticker.[179] We interrupted him playing in the children's playground. He didn't remember my name. So we pinched his for sixteen years.

Chandler
Our cat rescued from the wrong side of town, all long ginger squirm and fur. Named *Chandler* by Eleanor and Megan because of *Friends* on the telly, which we all loved.[180] When he ran out into the road, he couldn't be rescued again.

Tempuss[181]
Our real-time good-time fluffy bring-on-your-allergy cat, rescued by Megan and Eleanor from feral Gleadless. More black than white with white socks. She flaps in at five to seven every morning with stoats. Always pals with Maisie, they lie, stroke, poke, lick, ignore and scratch each other, like every other couple up our street.

Maisie
Our only-forever dog. She cost £56 from Thornberry, including her name. Manchester Terrier but not quite. Sleeps half the night with me, whatever half my listeners think.

---

179 His initials were TKR, therefore Ticker. But he was also a teacher who ticked your books. And ticked you off as well. People tried to call our Ticker Tiger and Tigger. I'd missed him out of these memoirs till Eleanor read them and told me, on the night my niece Steph and her Eric told us something even more important. We did wonder if Ticker might work as a name for them to use as well?
180 And my Eleanor adds, 'Chandler was a bit cleverer than you allow for, as we wanted to use the family name too.'
181 As in Tempus fugit = Time Flies, also Eleanor and Megan's idea.

Thirty-Three Years Later
The story so far.

Our Dave, born Feb 1st 1945, was the last of the Robinsons.

Mum spent the rest of her working life teaching at Sharrow Lane.

Dad did 49 years at the Town Hall, and ended up running the Council's insurance scheme. This mostly meant going out to visit teachers who had torn their trousers on broken school chairs, and ratepayers who had cracked their ribs on *mis-feased* pavements.

There wasn't much money, and we never moved from our red brick purple-roofed Laver House, however much Dad wanted to.[182]

We three boys went to Grammar School.

Geth went to King Edward's, and loved it. He had the highest IQ of his year, went on the science side, left after A levels, joined the Civil Service as a taxman, and stayed one till he retired.

Dave went to High Storrs, and failed his O levels, except for Art. He was the first to leave home, running off to sea at 17. Five years on, he went to Cardiff to take maritime degrees and then to London to be a lawyer and become the most academically qualified of anyone in all our families for ever.

I was next to leave when I went to Oxford, then London, though my parents always kept my bed.

Geth stayed at home till he was 30 odd, when he married child-bride Lorna and went up in the world, to Bents Green.

Mum and Dad retired, played bowls, acted, walked, gardened, holidayed and loved each other even more, once we weren't there.

*

---

182 Our Dave said, when he read these memoirs, 'As Geth and Lily were about the only professional couple on the Laverdene working continuously since around 1950 to 1984 I still cannot work out where all their incomes went. It wasn't on rent (I remember taking the rent book round to Nellie's with a £1 note in it) and even at the end Lily was only paying around £30 a week. It wasn't on furnishings, which remained virtually unchanged throughout. When did the yellow Formica kitchen table and stools replace the plywood table, which we used to play table tennis on? Up the Blades.'

And then - 29 sterile years after Dave - Geth and Lorna had Timothy Gethin who was afraid of helicopters, ate laburnum and was (is) cuddly, clever and musical. He went to Cambridge, and became religious, which just goes to show. He met Jane, had four children, Caitlin, Sam, Matty and Eilis, and once, grew a beard when he was performing as Joseph, but had to shave it off straight after.

Geth and Lorna also had Stephanie Lorna, who arrived just in time for my Dad to love unreasonably[183] because she was the first girl in the Robinson family since Aunty Olwen in the First World War. Steph was also cuddly, clever and musical. She was a Brownie, ballet dancer, Guide, Girl's Life Brigader, saxophonist, and banker. After which she went to Scarborough to be a teacher, and Buxton to be a Miss Robinson. She now lives happy ever after, in her own Laver House, though hers has a cellar, two lavs, and an orchard. She's married to a Blade, Eric Shaw, and lives with him and Ruby the second-best dog in Totley and….

*

A generation earlier, Our David married Susan at a wedding without drink in Cardiff, and my Dad made a speech no one asked for, about how Welsh we Robinsons are -

Ma'er coed yn llawn ffrwythau- dylen ni wneud rhywbeth a nhw!

Dave and Sue[184] then had three boys, Tomas, Anthony and Ben. One became a teacher, one a copper and one a banker. They all got married and have had zillions of dogs, and two daughters, all true Sheffield United-ites.

*

My Mum out-lived my Dad by 15 years.

Geth said in surprise one night as we were remembering her in the *Crown,* wasn't it funny how, whenever you turned up to see her, she always

---

183 Entirely reasonably, then and now.

184 Dave and Sue (not my Dave and Sue) were the invented middle-aged couple who were the target audience for BBC Local Radio a few years ago. They were chubby with glasses, and were enthusiastic about gardening, caravans and home improvement. They had gone to secondary moderns, and were young in their attitudes. He had a beard. BBC Local Radio output was directed towards them, especially towards Sue. Then the actor playing Dave on the posters and the DVDs died unexpectedly, and, worse, the audience figures suggested that middle-aged chubby, enthusiastic people like Dave and Sue not only died unexpectedly but also unexpectedly listened to commercial radio aimed at their children - because they were so young in their attitudes. That was the end of that Dave and Sue, really.

laughed and put the kettle on, and how everybody loved her?

When Geth himself died, which was shocking, everybody loved him too.

*

Meanwhile, I didn't get married - though you didn't not do in those days - and lived with my three at no 132.

*

Then Goronwy ran off to join the circus at 16, did a year of an acting degree at Bretton, then went back street-performing, cruising and producing variety shows, while living over the brush with Rosie in Sidmouth.[185] He took up the ukulele too.

Viv left 132 in 2001.

Eleanor went to Sussex to do Psychology, then Manchester to do Film, Theatre, and comedy. Megan went to Rose Bruford in Kent to sing, dance and act.

And one horrid August three years ago, after 23 years we emptied 132 and left it for other people to play their own games of happy families.

So to recap -

Dave was the last Robinson for 33 years. Then Geth, Dave and I had eight children. Our eight children so far have had six children.

(And we're still shaking that family tree.)

---

185 See footnote 189

Ticket to Ride
From a 2005 poetry blog I did but nobody noticed.

My forever pal got me a ticket to see
Bob Dylan
In a cinema in Brixton.
And we went and He was there and His hands
were too knobbly to play the guitar
And my pal waved his walking stick
And I cried because if even we can't be forever young
forever whoever can be?

But then next day my forever pal and I went without Bob
and trespassed in the school we taught at forty years ago.
We went into the classroom where I first heard Bob Dylan
(brought in by a naughty boy who traded him off for some homework)
and I borrowed the department's dansette without signing for it
and we turned the volume very low at playtime
when we should have been outside being shouted at to come in.

Well was I surprised to find all the kids still there in room 314
All the Johns and Pauline and Deborahs (and Tootses)
And Billys, Terrys, Janices, Lesleys, Colins and Lizzies.
And so were the flower posters on the wall
And the free verse
everywhere.

The best things would have been to write a poem about it
In
Free verse
Like we did in the sixties
When anything that got felt got written
And you could use capital letters whenever You wanted
and spill words according to your own rools
and the lines could go to any lengths With neither Rhyme Nor reason
and the daily mail said it was all the english teacher's faults
that society was unstreaming.

The poem could be called If Only
And that could refer to if-only-we-could-be-forever-young
And it could refer to something else, or something else as well as.

But that's what poetry can do -
Bob up and down like that.

Turning The Skellingtons
My parents had two secrets, remember?[186]

I'd not be the man I am today if it weren't for Norman Layland the milkman. So thank you Norman, and thank you Angela Treweek, the family historian who is often on the BBC digging up skeletons. For it was Angela who dug up Norman for me.

She'd already gone digging on my Mum's side and found things, e.g. on Census Night in 1901, my Grandy, Leon Gambetta Chandler aged 23 was lodging in a house on Burton Road in Carlton in Nottingham, and being described as a *Cart Builder.* And visiting that same house on that same night was my 22-year-old Nanny Chandler, then Gertrude E. Elvidge a *Mental Sick Nurse,* looking after May Hinckley aged 83.

The Census says he lodged ... she was visiting.

This was the night my Nanny and Grandy met?[187]

With her doing the talking of course. As in -

>   *Leon's a nice name I don't know any Leon's, it suits you ... I don't
>   have any gentleman callers at the moment actually.... Aren't you hot
>   in that cart-builder's smock?*

Dynasties starting, on Census night 1901? The Cart Builder and the Nurse? While Miss Hinckley slept?

>   *I like a moustache on a man. Bet it tickles? ... My father was a
>   Manager actually. I could do better than you. Still... Oh look where
>   your hand is now, Leon Gambetta!*

Leon and Gertrude did get it together, if not that night, and did live unhappily ever after as a result.

No, we don't really know that either.

How do you ever know about other people's love lives?

---

186 One of my readers points out that this section is too long, like people's stories of their family histories always are.

187 We don't know. That's the lesson of history. We never know, even when we know. All we can do is read the question carefully, and assume it contains the answer the examiner wants.

(How do you even know about your own?)

Either way, by 1911 Nanny and Grandy were married, and he was now a
Railway Clerk, and they were living at 2 Salisbury Rd, Unstone with three
daughters and a son aged 6, 5, 4, and 1.

The 4-year-old is my Mum, Lily.

Leon stayed a *Railway Clerk* for 35 years.

Family legend[188] is it that he was a member of the Independent Labour Party,
so didn't blackleg in the General Strike, so never got promotion, while his
scabbing brothers ended up in a big house above Sidmouth.[189] And one of
them became a (presumably Tory) Town Councillor.

But why would Nanny Chandler allow Grandy to go on strike? With all those
kids to feed? And let him send all those kids to Socialist Sunday Schools?
And how come she was always so keen on the Co-op for everything,
including his funeral?

Maybe she was one of those Labour people who recognise a good thing
when they see it, but just don't like other people very much?

She certainly didn't seem to like her husband very much, telling everyone,
including me as a kid, that she could have done better than him. I'd always
assumed he'd got her pregnant and ruined her life, and that this was her
revenge. But in fact her first child wasn't born until five years after Census
night, when they were already well-married.

So why had she settled for Leon Gambetta? The red-cheeked shiny man
who did watery watercolours and couldn't even beat his own grandchildren at
chess?

What was her hold on him? And what did it do to her kids to have a mother
who never let her husband have any money of his own? Who never let him
go out, except to work? Who made him garden in return for his St Bruno

---

188 Two other family legends. There was a Doctor William Chandler, maybe up Abbey Lane,
who treated poor people without charging them. And there was another William Chandler
who was a Chartist, hanged for poaching a sheep. My sort-of sister-in-law Lorna says there
was a bigamist William Chandler too, but there again she thinks she's a Wordsworth and a
Wedgwood.

189 Rosie Russell ran across and kissed Goronwy once, after he'd done a circus show in the
streets at the Sidmouth Folk Festival. We all fell in love with her too. She's from the famous
Russell family but they're another story. (Send for Angela.)

ration? Who bought and sold all their houses and caravans and dogs without even asking him? She was the one who organised the family so that each child went to college then came back and paid for their younger brothers and sisters to do the same.

If anyone didn't do what she organised, she cut them off, and everyone else had to cut them off as well. Lily's favourite brother Billy married. My Mum never saw him again. (And nor did we).

How could Nanny Chandler do that? What sort of model was she for her kids? And us? What was it that made her so bossy? Why did nobody stop her?

And why then did she shriek and claw and try to jump into her husband's grave at Abbey Lane when the Co-op were trying to bury him in 1957? What was she remembering about him then, long after his dementia had let him forget all about her?

Oh we're rattling the skeletons, now!

*

So what did Angela find next?

First she found my parents' full register office wedding certificate.

On it, Lily is 28, living at 55 Chantrey Road, and a spinster with no occupation, though in fact she had been a teacher for the previous six years.[190]

Leon Gambetta signs for her.

Uncle Trevor signs for my Dad.

There are no photos, or any evidence at all, that anyone else was at the wedding.

The Robinson and Chandler sides never met again, or even referred to each other in front of the grandchildren.

*

---

190 Mainly at Woodseats.

The full wedding certificate Angela found for February 1st 1935 also says that Dad is 34 and a Municipal Officer and -

> *Formerly the husband of Frances Edna Robinson formerly Parr, Spinster, from whom he obtained a divorce.*

Now, actually Dad had already told both Geth and me, separately, years apart, but, both times in the *Fleur de Lys,* that he'd been married before.

He never told us Frances Edna Parr's name but we'd found her in Aunty Gwenny's bad-tempered photo album at Milden Road. She sometimes wore glasses and sometimes just stood hanging round this handsome man who looked like Robbie Williams, with his pipe, tennis racket, motorbike and plus-fours.

There are no press cuttings about their almost-society wedding as in -

> *Wadsley Church School Headmaster's Handsome Athletic Motor Cycling Golfing Oldest Plus Foured Son Town Hall Wallah and Actor Marries Woman With Glasses*

Dad talked about Edna on only one other occasion, oddly again in the Fleur, and this time, even more oddly, to Viv, with me there, when she came to stay, in a separate room, one weekend early on in our relationship.

Fifty odd years after the divorce, I noticed, he still couldn't speak her name.

And that was about all I did notice.

*

But - cue Angela.

Looking for clues.

At Kew.

She found some more bones, and reported them one April Saturday, to the Family History Fair at Norfolk Park that I'd opened with a long speech, and probably the double entendre joke[191].

---

191 Or the one about the two Irish nuns on the Snake Pass when the Mother Superior tells the novice, when the Devil appears, 'Show him yer cross!' So the novice nun leans out and yells, 'Chuff off!' Or similar.

This time she'd found Dad's first wedding certificate.

On December 22nd 1927, Samuel Gethin Robinson married Frances Edna Parr of Riverdale Loxley, the 23-year-old spinster daughter of Francis Harry Parr, Manager Steel Works.

Dad was 28 and a Municipal Officer.

The witnesses this time were her father and Dad's brother Goronwy.

*

Angela had found a bit more, too.

On 20th September 1929 there was a Humble Petition from Samuel Gethin Robinson to the Probate Divorce and Admiralty Division for a divorce because the respondent Frances Edna Parr had -

> *frequently committed adultery with Norman Layland -*

then -

> *habitually lived and committed adultery with the said Norman Layland at 85 Clinton Avenue Blackpool from August 24th to September 1st 1929.*

The uncontested case of Robinson v Robinson and Layland was heard at Leeds Assizes, by which time Robinson and Layland were living together at 11A Primrose Avenue Sheffield, and Dad was living back at home with his Ma, at 112 Marcliffe Road.

Also established in the divorce papers was that Robinson and Robinson had previously lived at Riverside Cottage, Loxley. And that there was no *issue of the marriage.*[192]

*

So, what to make of it now?

---

192 Disappointing Angela, and lovers of family history. And me.

210

Well, divorce was rare, expensive[193] and shameful. Dad's marriage had lasted less than two years. The week in Blackpool to clinch it for the divorce suggests that it had all gone wrong much earlier - as in *frequently committed adultery.*

Why? And how much earlier? And how had Dad found out? Come back early from the Town Hall? Found them together at Riverside Cottage, Loxley? How hurt and humiliated was he? When did he decide to divorce her? How did it feel to go back to his Mum? How cross was Aunty Gwenny? And his Dad the Headmaster? And what about the two posh families who had got so close and gone on holidays together, on the snapshots, but could now never meet again?

Who was this Norman Layland, a more attractive prospect than the most wonderful man in the world ever?[194]

And how did it all this affect Dad's view of women, and marriage and things? And in due course, ours?

*

Thank you Angela

And thank you again Norman the milkman.[195] I'd not be living here happily ever after in Totley but for you.

*

There is, however, one more bit of family mystery left.

Only after my Mum died, and we were going through the papers yet again, did Geth and I realise she'd got married the day after she stopped working as a teacher, half way through the term. And that they'd then immediately come to Totley to our instant-for-rent redbrick house, nowhere near either of their parents or families.

And with no wedding pictures.

And no anniversaries.

---

193 The decree nisi was granted on 30 June 1930. Norman Layland had to pay my Dad's costs of £71.19.8. There are no Laylands in Sheffield on 192.com.
194 I told him the night he died. And it was true.
195 I don't suppose he was a milkman. Angela says I said he was, and I say she said he was.

Even when Dave was born - on their exact tenth wedding anniversary, on February 1ˢᵗ 1945.

*

By the mid 1930s both the Chandler and the Robinson families were falling apart.

The respectable Robinsons had suffered one divorce, and three early deaths - father, daughter and son. The oldest daughter was an invalid for life. The divorced oldest son was suddenly remarrying. The youngest daughter was having a long affair with a married man. The remaining son intended to join the war for democracy in Spain, as soon as his Ma said he could.

The aspiring Chandlers were crumbling as well. One daughter had failed as a nurse. One son had been banished. One had died. Another daughter was struggling. The youngest son was already odd. The father was about to retire on a negligible pension. There was a daughter still at school. And my Mum, who was the most stable, had suddenly left home for ever to go and live in Totley. With a divorced man.

*

Hard times in both families then, as my Mum and Dad had their wedding night on February 1ˢᵗ 1935 at 6 Laverdene Drive, and for the first time ever shared a bed.

Wondering who'd sleep on which side.

And who should say sorry first.

And what was going to happen next?

*

What did was Our Geth, born in Totley, or actually at a nursing home off Abbey Lane, on May 11ᵗʰ 1935.

Turn Your Wheels!
or
When Rony Maybe Met Sally

Maybe on a summer Saturday Oxford morning fifty years ago? Me on my sit-up-and-beg Raleigh with my scholar's gown tangling in the Sturmey Archer, and her in her purple Banbury School uniform, with a straw hat and an ice cream?

Or in the 70s, sitting opposite each other on London's Central Line tube from Mile End to Stratford, reading *The Alternative Theatre Handbook* and *Spare Rib?* When she was working in community health, and I was working in community theatre, and the whole East End was community mad?

Or at the 1978 biggest-ever womensrigthtochoose demo and march we both chose to be on from Hyde Park to Trafalgar Square?

Did we drink early 80's dandelion tea from the same mucky mug at the Commonground community café on the Wicker?

Or grin, both unmarried with kids, at Hattie Coppard's mocking wedding exhibition at the Mappin where couples were renewing vows in a marriage tent, not noticing the bride's cozzie was made of tampons?

We certainly camped out with all the other damp Saturday parents on the dazzling *Crucible* carpets, getting quick drinks in, while our cloth kit dungareed kids slid down the lunchtime slide that wasn't allowed.[196]

We clowned all day in Sheffield on Beano Friday, when Sally was Dilly the Pierrot in the Peace Gardens and I was Rony everywhere, being given the most wonderful time, just because I'd written a novel.

And she did phone me on the BBC to get a listener to lend her a *bone fide* holder to hold her *bone fide* Heath Robinsons Izal toilet roll[197] for a *bone fide* exhibition.

We definitely did a BBC interview about her telling stories in the woods. And I heard her being noisy with her street band on Chesterfield May Days.

---

196 But gave more pleasure to more Sheffielders than any play, snooker or musicintheround in the Crucible, all put together, ever did.
197 And years later she did a bone fide Radio 4 documentary about it that won a Sony Bronze in 2010.

We were both at Tim and Jane's sunfilled Whirlow wedding, too, for she was squeezing with *Airs and Graces* the all-women's ceilidh band, and Our Dave and I were dancing with each other, for the first time ever.

Without knowing, Sally and I also enrolled simultaneously with the *Maureen Birtle's Driving School* above the bridal underwear shop at Heeley. Both our Maureen Birtleses turned out to be ex-steel worker George Eyre of Dronfield, so we squirmed in the same driver's seat for a year, whenever he growled at us to –

> *Set your gas!*
> *Find your biting point!*
> *Turn your wheels!*

George reported us to each other too, telling us that *Old Sally* or *Old Rony* was doing better than we were, even when we didn't know who Old Sally and Old Rony were.

But we passed.

And time passed.

*

And before you can say Jack Robinson, here we are sitting in the Friday night *Stag* on Psalter Lane. It's the pub Charley Peace went to just before the Banner Cross Murder. We talk about the Lantern. And then Oxford, dandelion tea, Banbury, community, Stratford, the other Stratford, women's rights to choose, Peace, beer, marriage, peace, common ground, the Peace Gardens, communes, men, the Mappin, Mappin's Ale, the saxophone, Common Ground, Staithes, women, non-violent education, the Beano, the impossibility of relationships, where Heeley becomes Meersbrook, Dads, the BBC, the NHS, kids, stags, dungarees, slides, Izals, storytelling, squeezing, rambling, dancing – and Maureen Birtles.

Then time started passing again.

*

We started writing together, once we were together.

Last Loves was the first of four Radio Four plays. It was a result of a tiny leaflet from the BBC saying they were interested in new writing from Yorkshire because not enough people here watch BBC 1. It had to be about some *hidden injustice*. It was going to be part of a big scheme with big money involving telly and regional theatre.

Out of it came our little play with songs, and little money, about love in old age. The hidden injustice we'd suggested as a result of work Sally had been doing in old people's homes, was that it might not be easy to have a proper love life in such places, especially if you were starting out on a new relationship, and you weren't as young as you were, and might need some help?

And what if you wanted sex in old age? With someone new? With yourself?

Especially if with old age came this *disinhibition* (a new word for me), and new needs? In no home we visited was it possible to get a double bed if you suddenly needed one. Or even much privacy. We met progressive carers who were as uneasy about it as we were becoming.[198]

We'd found our hidden injustice.

We also found a great place for dementia sufferers in Bradford where the clients were taken off the anti-depressants as soon as they arrived. We liked the playfulness there, and the way people interconnected again and were able to laugh at their own funny behaviour. And it was there one afternoon that we met *Kate* and *Bob* – our lovers with dementia - and wondered what it's like for husband *Paul* who has to visit a wife who is knocking off a fellow patient, disinhibitedly, and probably thinking he is her husband anyway?

I wrote up the story.

Sally cut and pasted the voices and made songs from them, to be sung by real older people.

The BBC Drama people encouraged us, though we didn't need much encouragement, and then luckily we got Pauline Harris in Manchester to direct us.

> **BOB**
> You get less jabber with men.
> **PAUL**
> Kate doesn't jabber does she?
> **BOB**
> Kate?

---

198 The most unexpected carer we met wondered if clients should be helped to use prostitutes, if they wanted. Maybe that's the Gold we missed.

PAUL
Kate? Sits here sometimes?
BOB
Right.
PAUL
You know her. Kate?
BOB
I'd recognise her, I think. Yes. You know her do you, this - who?
PAUL
Kate.
BOB
Kate. Who was she?
PAUL
She was my wife.
BOB
Don't know her.
PAUL
She might look a little like your wife but she doesn't have to.
BOB
My wife never worked to a system. My wife's dead. I think. Isn't she?

This touching play by Rony Robinson and Sally Goldsmith
successfully confronts the taboo of sex in old age though the bawdy
songs are at times queasily over informative
Stephanie Billen (The Observer)

Extraordinarily touching bittersweet drama. What really gave the
play legs were the songs especially written for the piece by Sally
Goldsmith.
'I'm Ernestine Flowers I don't like to complain,
So I sit in the window by my counterpane…
It's no use crying what good does that do
So I'll see you next week for an hour or two'
- sang one of the inmates in a tremulous but still clear voice and it
wrung the heart.
Sue Arnold (The Observer)

*

Mummies and Daddies was our next Pauline collaboration with Sallysongs.
It told of Chloe and Jacko who are given pretend babies from school for the
weekend, to discourage them from having early sex. They travel across the
city in a bus with them, on a Sunday, to give them a day out, and then have
early sex in a church, in Dore.

CHLOE (V/O)
And we - do it. Still talking and drinking mostly.
Babies are quiet for once and all, but all time I'm thinking shush,
please, don't cry now.
But it's not like you thought.
It doesn't take long, for a start.
I never knew like. In films and on telly. How long's it take?
But, after all the talk about it. And the thinking about it.
You just - do it.
And after.
I'm glad I done it. I think.
Yeah, am.
There are worse lads than Jacko.
And I do fancy him.
And he fancied me.
Must have. Right fancied.

*

In our third play the *Women of an Uncertain Age* help each other to be reborn
in middle life, with Sallypoems this time. The Methodist Minister's partner
Heather leaves him and goes to be with the birds. Cleaner Kat, with husband
and family, takes up music and falls in love with her piano teacher. Councillor
Clare runs off to London's Greenwich Park to find a lost rebel schoolboy love,
as the impossible suddenly isn't.

CLARE
When the sun bleeds we will run to the prickle bushes without a
word, like on the day of the strike, on the best day ever of all my life,
when we both said no and then both said yes.

*

Pauline play number four is *49 Letters*, without any Sallyatall.

It tells of two workers in the Sheffield history archives, David and Julia. They
love each other but daren't say so because they have partners and, much
more important, children. And there is also a teenage daughter struggling
with separated parents, and the new boy friend who turns out to be gay. The
film *Sleepless in Seattle* comes into it as well, as in -

> *Destiny is something we invented because we can't stand the fact
> that everything that happens is accidental.*

The Guardian compared it to Poliakoff.

At the end, in York on Christmas Eve, it begins to snow -

> **DAVID**
> If you took your glasses off I could say you're beautiful.
> **JULIA**
> Take yours off first.
> **DAVID**
> I'm too shy.
> **JULIA**
> Will you give me a kiss please and then we can say goodbye.
> **DAVID**
> With or without glasses?
> **JULIA**
> …With.
>
> *They kiss*
>
> **JULIA**
> Without.
>
> *They kiss.*

These four Pauline plays would make a nice box set.

They are quietly experimental comedies[199], political love stories for the ignored, with small hopeful endings.

The people who helped us make them, especially the 'real' people we talked to or whose stories we pinched, deserve some of the medals we got, especially for *Last Loves,* which made us flavour of the month for a few days at the BBC.

---

199 Who said it - not me - but the difference between comedy and tragedy is mostly about when you decide to stop. And in comedies people usually don't die, but in tragedies they have to. Oh, and you don't have to be quite so posh to be taken seriously in comedies.

Three Weddings and Some Funerals

I've been working for ages on a novel that started at my nephew Tim's perfect wedding at Whirlow, though some uncles drank too much even then. There was fire-juggling over the Bride, several vicars who sat down to lunch, and at the end of a perfect day, dancing to the all-women's folk band.

In my novel, things aren't so perfect.

The uncles drink even more. One falls for a member of the band. An aunt leaves her marriage. There are storms, ghosts, dogs, a vicar who disgraces himself in the bushes, and a bride and groom who go up on the Moors to separate because their wedding chauffeur was once her lover.

By the time the first drafts of the novel were finished, it was my niece Steph's wedding at Tankersely, which was just as perfect, though there were people not there who should have been. There were still some uncles drinking, plus juggling, dancing, ghosts and sunshine. There was even a vicar to argue with, plus a swim before breakfast.

Tim and Steph's weddings were both great fun. I hope my own will be, once I can work out who should die as a result of it.

*

For, from the very first page of my wedding novel, within days of Tim's original, I always had a sentence saying something like -

> *By the midnight of this wedding day, there will have been five orgasms and a death.*

Sometimes *Five Orgasms and a Death* has been the title. At other times it's been *April Loves* and *There I Met a Monkey.*

What with Tim's and Steph's and mine, there's not been a day for ten years that I've not thought about weddings, and the laughs, love, sex and death that go with them.

*

Yet, really, I don't believe in weddings.

When hassled, I say it's because I like women too much.

Which might mean I can't be monogamous.

Or it might mean (which is what I mean it to mean) that marriage is a patriarchal institution which (historically) diminishes the role of women by, suggesting (e.g. by them being 'given away' by one man to another man, and by them then changing their man's surname for another man's surname, and by them never speaking at their own weddings) that women are men's chattels.

Marriage is, I also mean to say, an insult to all those who think there are other ways in which people can live and love, without needing the permission of church and state. Nor should the church and state ration our love lives.

Oh and everyone who gets married makes it harder for anyone who doesn't, or can't.

*

So, I've never got married myself. And I won't, though I've noticed some of my ex-hippy pals have taken to late-onset marriages, because of pensions or maybe just to zhush[200] up their bedroom lives. Or because they want to join the grown-ups at last and let everyone know how wrong they were when they were young and hopeful.

But believed in or not, weddings are still fun to be at, full of dancing and unexpected people, ghosts, dressing ups and carnival. They are licensed over-excited sexy days of fun, even if you are at the back, crying -

> *Don't! It's patriarchy!*

Or -

> *It should have been me!*

You remember the weather at all the weddings you've ever been to, and what the food was like, and if there was anything to drink. You remember who was still alive then, too.

*

---

200 How would you spell it then?

And you remember all the surrealism.

Like the bride who called Peter Shears on the radio, to find out what her consumer rights were after her wedding dress ripped at the altar and the congregation saw her bottom.

Or Alan's wedding where there were rotating clothes pegs on the back of everyone's posh clothes all the long nobby afternoon.

Or Dave's when we went from sweet blue sherry, small white sandwiches and cream horns direct to the top hotel in Southampton for bony game soup, steak tartare with deep red wine and summer pudding with quadruple cream, all served at the same time, so that we could immediately catch the train, and bubble and squeak our way back to London together, for the honeymoon.

At Alan and Jenny's, the food was six meatballs on a silver tray.

At Francis and Mark's Derbyshire Irish one, everyone wrote poems on the napkins.

At one I went to, the registrar thought Andrew was Andrea.

And what about the steeplechasing across vast lawns to catch the waiter for tiny lumps of scorched fish on silver trays, at Tom's? Or the unprepared speech at Anthony's by the uncle who seemed to have been drinking, and was giving no indication that he was about to stop?

At the first lesbian wedding I went to, a cry went up at the end -

You may now kiss the brides!

Or take Miles'[201] wedding. I'd so wanted to be his Best Man and I have been resentful for decades that he'd not asked me, because I love him this side of adultery. I said so at last, last year in their flat in Valencia, and told him how disappointed and jealous I had been for 40 years. Ingrid said yes, but you *were* the Best Man. She found the photos - and I was.

Weddings punctuate our lives and remind us of the power of love and the frailty of memory, and the need for forgiveness. They also suggest life can be better.

---

201 Miles Roddis, Durham University linguist, British Council polyglot, cyclist, Lonely Planet travel writer, pal from King Ted's times, where we shared among other things the Essay prize and each think the other should have won it. Or the other way round.

I said some of that in my too-long speech at Steph's wedding, which started with the brightly- coloured trousers Eric first saw me in[202] and ended with the *double entendre joke,* which was a mistake, as usual.

*

And funerals?

Well, you remember them too.

You wonder why him? Why her? And why this way, and why now? And, of course, who's next?

You remember the dead person more sharply than ever, only to have to leave them on their own, because you're off to the first party of the rest of your life they'll not be at.

You'll pretend, once there, to be celebrating their life, but everyone is a generation too old, at a wedding gone monochrome.

*

In Ecclesall Church, the Dore Male Voice Choir blazered away for Our Geth's funeral and I'd like them to blazer away for me too, if there are any of us left by then.

Rev Jockel of All Saints did my Dad, and got uneasy when the freemasons turned up to do whatever they do to dead brethren - presumably roll up their trouser legs.

Frank Abel, Goronwy's old headmaster, did the Humanist one for my Mum and made everyone laugh by imitating her offering everyone a cup of tea.

*

The best funerals I've been to lately include a woodland burial, with bananas, accordion, and a coach trip. And one with live Morris music.

Fred Pass's was good, as brave and full of love as he was, with *Fields of Gold* to break your heart.

---

202 In the earliest days of their love story, in the lost petrol station at Bushey Wood, Eric says, 'Look at that chuff in those trousers!' Steph replies, 'That's my uncle!'

Capstick's was packed into the cold ugly church in Wentworth, but somewhere far off in the chancel he was still young and singing, and we all applauded as they carted him off to his next gig.

Dave Sheasby's funeral was massive, with his kids telling his stories even better than he did, and a slide show to show how badly he dressed.

Sally's Mum's writing about her childhood made up most of her two homemade funerals and meant she was young again at both.

Dave Godin, the anarchist cineaste, organised his funeral so that his Dalmatian bitch was loosed into the crem as it started. His guests included a coachload of Northern Soul enthusiasts in hats, all South Yorkshire's armchair anarchists, and an ex-lover explaining in farm language why Dave personally so identified with the Devon Donkey Sanctuary who were to benefit from the proceeds of his funeral.

Uncle Trevor's funeral at Blackpool had no congregation except for Dave, Geth and me. The funeral director made a speech even though we'd asked him not to, about how, while he didn't know Mr Robinson, he had had the honour of burying Mrs Robinson, once.

*

And my funeral?

When I left 132, the lawyers said I could include instructions for it, to be kept by them with my first ever Will, at no extra expense, in case anything ever happened.

So on the understanding that it was at no extra expense, and that nothing ever would happen, I wrote my funeral, like Mr Toad.

It started with a pre-recorded speech by me, saying-

> *I'd like to be burned, at Hutcliffe Wood where my parents and brother went before.*
>
> *As jolly a coffin as possible.*
>
> *Autoharp on top.*

Then there were quotes from Brecht, and a detailed running order in which Goronwy had to juggle and Eleanor and Megan had to play music.
And -

> *Bob Dylan should sing, probably Forever Young.*

> *The other Dylan should be in there too, maybe Do Not Go Gentle.*

> *And near the very end the very last pages of Winnie the Pooh.*

I included instructions for themed speeches -

> *Oxford - The Sunken Quad Days!*

and -

> *Why 77 Women Weep Today!*

There were other instructions too -

> *Everyone to wear something red !*

> *Dogs welcome!!*

> *There must be a quiz!!!*

I think now, though, I'd like to be a bit less important at it.

But there's plenty of time yet. Isn't there? [203]

---

203 But I would like a matt white cardboard coffin for everyone to write on like when kids have their wrists in plaster. A newly-bereaved husband told me on the radio this summer that he'd done a deal with his wife to have one of those, and he'd already written on hers as promised — 'This way up.'

What Was Stuck On The Pinboard In The Kitchen Before It Fell Down

Post-modern Man

Rony is what he is
Though what he was as well
And what he will be
Even if he won't
Isn't
Or wasn't

11. Who's Been Talking?

When Rony Met Rony

Right, so how do I start?

Just start.

How do you start?

I just start.

But I make sure I have the name of the person I'm about to interview written down in front of me.

Why?

Because there was a newsreader once, who began -

This is BBC Radio Sheffield and here is the 11 o' clock news read by -

Who?

He forgot.

Don't you write down what you're going to ask as well?

I heard a *Woman's Hour* presenter years ago saying the only way she could make herself listen was not to have her questions ready, except for the first one, just in case.

And is that what you do?

No.

What do you do?

I don't have any questions ready, if I can help it. Richard and Judy never did either.

What's your worst interview in 26 years?

Arthur Scargill, this year. The papers had been talking about his two homes. I've wanted for ages to do one more long interview with him - we often met on

228

the radio in the 80s and 90s,and he is such an important and puzzling figure -and a good radio DJ actually. This time he was suddenly on the phone. Everyone in the newsroom stopped to listen. I couldn't focus it at all.

Give us some tips on doing it right then?

Suddenly change your line of questioning without warning by saying moving on or if we can just turn to.

Stop the interview surprisingly, while you're still winning.

Don't listen to other people's tips.

If we could just turn to you, then? You're *Mr Nice Guy* usually but then you suddenly have a go at someone?

I think it's my job to have a go at the people with power and do whatever I can to empower the powerless.

Naff or what?

All right, but when Radio Sheffield began it was part-financed by the Council, and Councillor Ironmonger (such a name) said he wanted to support it because it would enable the people of Sheffield to conduct their own business in their own language.

Is that *naff or what* too?

A bit. Has it so enabled them?

Sometimes.

The Miners Strike of course.

World Student Games.

Hillsborough Disaster, of course.

The Floods.

But also in all the moments every day when we speak and listen to each other. Recognise ourselves in each other. Respect each other's courage. Are less lonely. Laugh togeth-

So moving on, give us some tips from a master with a proud record of 26 years of broadcasting without a mistake?

You're only saying that.

The great Martin Dawes said it in the *The Star* actually.

You asked him to actually.

Moving on, tips?

Do it live.

Face to face.

Eye contact.

Cry.

Be there.

Laugh.

Didn't you get told off for laughing?

Yes.

More tips?

Know what song you're going to go to as soon as the interview's over. If in doubt say it's *The Foundations*.

Ask the same question again sometimes.

Ask one question nobody else would have done.

If your interviewee's boring it's your fault.

You can't believe that?

Almost always I can.

Oh, and stories are more interesting than opinions and most people share their opinions by stories anyway.

And listeners remember stories.

Carry on maestro!

Ask women the questions men usually get asked and men the women's questions[204].

Shut up sometimes.

Say chuff every so often to improve your street cred.

Interrupt somet-

If we can turn now to the question of BBC bonuses? I expect you've had your share?

One. £500, three years ago.

Why did you get it?

I don't know.

What you do get paid?

32 thousand a year before tax. On six month contracts, 25 days holiday.

That's not bad for a three-hour working day, though?

No.

Do the other presenters get more?

I don't know.

Do the other presenters get more?

I don't know.

But there again you haven't won many prizes, have you?

---

204 Kate Linderholm's brilliant insight, after 26 years.

I ran-up as Sony UK Local Broadcaster of the year last century.
And Neil Grant and I were nearly the winning local-radio-garden-phone-inners in a small garden gardening magazine last year.

You also got your honorary doctorate from Sheffield Hallam University for your services to the arts and broadcasting. Because that's why you refer to yourself as *Doctor* half the time, to impress us isn't it? And you made an enormous speech in the City Hall when you were awarded it even if three thousand people were getting anxious to be back in the pub?

I was tipped for one at Sheffield University the same year, but I was blackballed after that.

Moving on then, I expect you have your own BBC office, BBC secretaries and runners, and car parking?

None of the above.

I also don't have a locker, clothes peg, desk or computer.

I have a pigeonhole where I keep my muesli and a fleece for outside broadcasting that still says -

There's a sparkle in the air!

Moving on, beer or wine?

Red wine these days, unless it's very real real beer.

You still do any writing these days?

What do you think this is? I've also got two nov-

List five shows that make you the writer you are today, then?

1. *The Last Resort* - Green Ginger (Old Fudge Factory, Beaumaris 1985)
2. *Oh What A Lovely War!* - Theatre Workshop (Theatre Royal Stratford East 1968)
3. *Under Milk Wood*[205]- King Edward VII Literary and Debating Society (Room 46, 1958)

---

[205] It was at King Edward's that the classics master poked me in the stomach and warned me if I didn't do something about my Ancient Greek I'd never be a real writer and I'd end up like Dylan Thomas instead of TS Eliot. And I did.

4. *The Arabian Nights* - Shared Experience (Crucible Studio 1976)
5. *Mother Goose* - Frank Randle[206] (Lyceum1947)

All a bit old aren't they? But moving on - what do you have on your iPod?

Abba, Bob Dylan, masses of Mozart masses, Richard Thompson, the Lindsays, Sugarbabes-

United or Wednesday?

There's only one Sheffield team.

Tell me about Crosspool?

Saturday fortnightly youth dances at St Columba's.

With a band and pass outs, the palais glide and the girls excuse me.

Constant Grant be our guide!

Get away with a slow quickstep in the foxtrot.

The girls from Grange Grammar know some of our names.

Read the *Green Un* and pretend we've not noticed them.

Wait for the cha-cha, no one knows how to do that.

French kiss till you can't move in gardens on Ringstead Crescent.

Swing on the outdoor swings till they snap and you splash together into the goldfish lakes of Westover Road.

Smoke Olivier tipped above the fish shop, drink halves in *The Sportsman* and fall in love without ever doing much about it, knowing that even the much you don't do everyone will know about by playtime on Monday.

Oh Jean and Bill, Judy, Geoff, Gill and Dave Tom, Olive, Jacko, Barry, Seamus, Miles, Johnny, Fritz -

And we mustn't forget singing *Ramona* to Mrs Garside's piano in the Friday night *Ranmoor* and -

---

206 **Cinders**   Oh Buttons Buttons! Thwarted again!
   Buttons (Randle)   Ne'er mind lass! Open winder!

Who else mustn't you forget?

Norman and Mary Wilson.

Who are they and why do they matter?

They're cyclists and recyclists in Widnes. They read books to each other in bed and they'll do that with this one, and I am suddenly nervous. I've tried all sorts of tricks to hide me, but I suddenly feel like Pamela Green in *Naked as Nature Intended*. Reading my life in bed sounds fun though? I can hear Malcolm and Sandra laughing again. And Max in his come-to-bed Villa strip, trying to do my Yorkshire voice for giggling Chrissie. Alan and Jenny rosy cheeked again. There's something going on in a siesta in Valencia. Who's Danny reading to? There are four-in-a-bed on the Laverdene, but who's reading? And -

Moving on, how do you, as a trained Oxford historian with a second-class honours degree, place your own life in its historical context?

Born in a decade of war and austerity, I have the longest life expectation of any child ever born to any ordinary family in Britain in history.

I was born 16 months too late to ever have to do any compulsory military service, and was the first kid on either family who ever went to Oxford, or university at all, I think.

I am richer than any of my family ever was on either side, though I'm not rich. Think of the improvements in medicine.

And food.

Or think of the inventions since 1950 - e.g. I have the complete Shakespeare on my phone.

And Rock and Roll!

I'm lucky enough to be young enough to be flexible about all that, and not to keep wanting the good old days back.

I was lucky to be born in an era of increasing disbelief in religion and authority - when you could be optimistic about making things better all over the world.

I grew up just in time for dry cleaning, washing machines, deodorants and stuff galore to stop you smelling like everybody in history must have.

Women got freer in my lifetime. The pill and the second wave of feminism altered permanently the relationship between men and women.

I didn't meet a black person till I was 17.

Gays used to go to prison.

Things have got slowly more diverse, and interesting and colourful.

I became a teacher just as comprehensive schools were starting, and corporal punishment dying, and an English teacher at exactly the time English teaching was transforming.

I became a playwright at the time a properly subsidised Arts Council was forcing new plays everywhere.

I had kids when parenting could be done differe-

Favourite colour?

Red though I look better in pale purple.

Favourite film? *The Railway Children* of course!

Of course

Favourite Shakespeare? *Julius Caes-*

Winters Tale maybe? I'm too old for tragedy.

You mean you're not 37?

I have been.

How do you vote, not that it's not a bit chuffing obvious?

Three different parties in the last three elections.

But I believe exactly what I believed and disbelieved at 16, only more so. The world is unfairl-

Are you or have you ever been a member of a para-military political organisation?

I was Red Sixer with the First Totley Cub Scouts.

Oh and I was for a short time a card-carrying member of Troops Out, and once kissed Pat Arrowsmith the pacifist in a pub in New Cross, after a meeting.

You like pubs don't you?

Not as much as I did. One of the great developments of my lifetime has been cheap home drinking, especially good wine at a fiver a bottle. Oh and real coffee, everywhere. And -

Thank you.

That it?

Yes, soz. Stationality rules. Time for *Build Me Up Buttercup* by The Foundations

Wel, Bobo Bach, Mae'r Ceir Tramor 'Ma'n Rhyfedd – Does Dim Periant Yn Y Car![207]

Beaumaris, Anglesey, (says the on-line guide book) holiday town on the Menai Strait with Victorian gaol and courthouse. At the gaol, visit the condemned cell or experience the darkness of the punishment cell. Handle chains and fetters last worn by prisoners a century ago.

So, *bore da,* 1980 and here we are in the hot Whit sun with my two pink little girls in one pushchair guzzling Cadwalladddwallwallawallawalla-wallawallawallars ice cream by the Castle before we go off to paint pigs under a rainbowed mountain.

Dymo'r sisop sy'n gwerthu hafen la

*

And look, it's 1952 and an old leaky 1930s Daimler, all fluid flywheel and no gear stick, is purring in the slicing Welsh rain. We are 51, 45, 16, 11 and 6, rumbling down Castle Street, all damp five of us, dripping past two chemists, two paper shops, two butchers, two bakers, one antique shop, one castle, church, prison, courtroom, pier, six pubs - and knowing even then, even now, that we'll be coming back here for ever.

*

And it's 1963. I am 21 in the AB button phone box next to the *Bulkely Arms* trying to hear Oxford over the cackling morning Welsh and their cockling mourning seagulls and find what BA I've just got, with very early beer to follow either way.

*

Goronwy is 12 years old magicking women from flowers in White Lion Square in front of the yellowing *Museum of Childhood* that we don't need because we bring our own.

*

---

207 We go to Beaumaris for one week every year, and it's different every time. In between we remember it differently, but all at the same time.

It's also 1968 and Dad is diving into *Willi the Welch* the *Welsh Bookie* just above the church (where he never dives) to put a couple of bob each way on *Saratoga Skiddy* in the 3.30 at Wincanton.

Ond dyna I gyd sy gyda fi yn y banc!

*

Tim is in short trousers still, 31 years later. He scuffles his sandals up The Road with No Name and tells our story of *The Road With No Name.* That Road leads to the Prison that closed for business in 1873, so if you've not been treadmilled or executed by then, you never can be. But you can still visit the condemned cell, experience the darkness of the punishment cell and handle chains and fetters last worn by prisoners a century ago.

*

And look! It's the best of times. That's Charles Dickens in 1832, come like us to wonder why Wales's biggest door is here, opposite the *Cottage Café* where, look, my Mum is treating us to fat slices of three-layered strawberry cream cake out on the crumbling balcony above the peckish seagulls.

*

That's us, there too! On the edge of the murky oblong sea-water pool, and Mum and Dad are already too old to be in swimming costumes, with their white goosy legs. Dive in before anyone can see it happening to us too.

*

And here we all are concentric as the sea is long, on the colonial battlements looking up *Welsh in a Week* to work out what they've been saying there for ever -

Cusanu?
Na!
Oes!
Mmmm.

*

And over there! Look! It's us, trudging out of the wet into the Old David Hughes School to see an exhibition of lamb.

*

Sit at this tiny bench now on the tiniest beach by the tiniest pier in Wales, though once there was a café out there with Horlicks, when great liners sailed from Liverpool with John Lennon on them. Now there is only air and flounder. Lily and Young Geth are just finishing the *Daily Telegraph* crossword, as the sun winkles over Snowdon, and decides not to bother again today.

*

And no thank you, *prynhawn da,* but we're not queuing for the *Saucy Blodwen* to sail round Puffin Island this afternoon. We haven't queued or sailed for 57 years, and Puffin Island's not flying anywhere. Look back instead down the tunnel past the best *pysgodyn* in Wales, opposite the worst *dynion* in Wales, and if it isn't we'll wait till we get back to England anyway. Look up the Pentraeth Road curling through the emptied Baron Hill estate with its tumbled mansion and hidden barking farms in the woods.

*

Look! There! Eleanor and Megan and Steph hand-in-hand among the rabbits, telling true stories including *Lorna And The Naughty Horse* and *What John Did In The Pool.* Turn round and tell the stories again. *The Naughty Horse and Lorna,* and *In The Pool, John Did What?*

*

Lily and I sit uncomfy and wet in the *Canoflan* quite early one poetry morning listening to RS Thomas reciting in a bad temper and raincoat.

> *You are old now; time's geometry*
> *Upon your face by which we tell*
> *Your sum of years has with sharp care*
> *Conspired and crossed your brow with grief*

Bolllloccs!

*

Sue is speaking 1994 Welsh at Dave, by the Old Courthouse, while he films her with his Pâthé News Camera. He simultaneously makes the first mobile call ever on his huge phone all the way to his London lawyer's office, where he is so important that they need to know where he is all the time. Even if he doesn't know what day it is half the time. And doesn't need to. And nor do any of us, on this one week forever.

*

Time soon for rounders and French cricket. And shared dogs and picnics and the greatest walk in the Welsh world, to Llandrwyn Island. Then if the sea and the wind are kind and we still aren't any older, onwards to the display of *Lifeguard Cottages* in the last lifeguard cottages before Ireland.

*

Stroll past *Ena's the News,* that Dave still thinks is *Edna's the Nudes,* then past the dog bone and cat flea stuff shop that was, and the *Tudor Rose* that even more was, old and rosy as the Tudors, opposite the chemist where, look, I am spending half my holiday money on *Valderma,* for the girls back in Crosspool. Climb up into the Old Town Hall and buy late slate birthday presents saying *To the Best Mum in the World* in Welsh for mothers and others who shouldn't have birthdays in August, always drawing attention to themselves.

*

Gethin and Lorna still young enough to be married are sharing *bara briths* in the Castle Bakery, and so are Eric and Steph, while Tomas the teacher, Welsh on both bare backsides, slithers down the steps into the bowling green, with Ben the Bank and Bruv the Bobby close behind. Followed by the *plentyn* yet to come

*

Oh come back again to Wales, the land of your fathers!

Ynys Mon, Mother of Wales!

Fall into your mother's arms!

And the *Sailors Arms.*

And the *Liverpool Arms*

And the *Bold Arms*

And the *Bulkely Arms*

Get slaughtered in the *George and Dragon*

Take the *Bull* by its *pels*

But –

Nos da now. Nos. I'll enter the *White Lion's* den on my own, in case Ceinwen is waiting there, like she did once, llong ago.

Awn ni I gyd I'r traeth heno!

*

The Beaumaris Prize Silver Band marches off the sunset pier, straight into the strait, leaving minims and crochets dancing among the kittiwakes. There are children laughing themselves to sleep on the sheepish hills where you can sometimes still nearly see in the fine rain tiny whitewashed *Tynnyymmynyyds,* with Mrs Griffin still making porridge in her wooden Aga, and Mr Griffin still hugging his bony cow in the stony yard in the *Anglesys* we first loved three childhoods ago, on the gull flown hills smelling of peat fire and Welsh sheepdog.

Mae'n well I my fiynd adre nawr!

X Marks the spot

Actually, Donna Hartley didn't agree. But she wouldn't have would she? It was her husband Bobby Knutt what done it.

What he'd done was, I was walking Maisie in Gilly Woods and I got a call saying would I do him a favour. He was booked for a charity gig at this Rotherham school, months away, but he'd just been offered work on a cruise ship. If he sent me a crate of red wine would I do it for him? Tempted, and remembering how Bobby helped when our friend Mike Kay from the *Crucible* was having such a desperate time, I said I would if I could and I'd check the diary when I got home.

And I did, and I could, so I said I would. And I did.

I didn't expect the wine, but it came, and I drank it.

And two months later I died.

*

Charity prevents me naming any more names.

But imagine me arriving at this snooty hotel in Rotherham, for a function with raffle and live entertainment, to raise funds for a school.

The taxi costs me 25 quid.

I know nobody in the welcoming party and nobody knows me. They aren't sure what I'm going to be doing but meanwhile I am free to buy myself a drink and mingle.

Well I can't drink, though everyone else obviously can, because I don't drink when I'm working, and charity gigs are more work than working is.

So I just mingle with orange juice, introducing and reintroducing myself to the same people. I tell them I know Dave Brennan the Rotherham jazzer, and have met Jive Bunny. I butt in, suggesting the Millers could do better with a better defence. I mention Michael Cooke and Spencer the Rover, and they say sorry, but aren't they supposed to be dead?

An hour and a half later, my fillings sizzling with the orange, I am seated next to Donna Hartley, which is good, and the five hundred of us slowly enjoy vegetable and bromide soup, water, Rotherham chicken, something with custard and a long bathroom break.

When proceedings resume it becomes clearer what I am not doing.

I am not doing the MC-ing because this popular local bloke already is.

I am not doing the raffle because there isn't one.

I am not doing the charity auction, because there isn't one.

I am not doing the big cheque and the photograph with my thumbs up because there isn't a photographer, and who'd want my photo if there was.

I'm not singing the *Titanic* song because this little girl already is, and is already sinking to enthusiastic applause.

Somebody creeps over, hands me a hand-mike and whispers that it shouldn't be too long, we are overrunning a bit. It's going very well, Tony. And don't go anywhere near the speakers, Tony, or there'll be the most godalmighty feedback. Just tell them some jokes for forty minutes or so. While the tables are cleared for the disco!

I tell Donna I don't know any jokes. She says Bobby doesn't do blue.

A defeated contestant from a cable TV talent show plays The *Dream of Olwen,* and loses again.

Charitable people stand up like Quakers one after the other to give lukewarm thanks to people I've never heard of.

There are several hours of this.

I need the lav after all the orange but I daren't go because I know I'll never dare to come back if I do.

I borrow a pen and write some shaky notes on a doily - *Capstick* and *double entendre* and *Grindleford* and *bloody bloody Knutty.*

*

And this is when I die.

For I am suddenly spotlit and pointed at, mispronounced and announced without even the safety net cry of -

He's doing it for charity!

*

Now, I've made a chuff of myself in public before.

Charity auctions, for example, are always a shambles. The more they raise, the more shambolic they are, because the bourgeoisie like filling themselves with drink before they then buy things they don't need with money they shouldn't have. They treat the charity auctioneer like a servant, and bay and scoff when he tries to be funny and tries to sell them bargains he could never afford himself.

I've done loads of openings of things, and holdings-up of cheques and thumbs, and speakings-up for Yorkshire, Wales, Public Service Broadcasting, Lifeboats and all.

I've been snubbed without fee by Alan Sillitoe and Cat Stevens. And Benjamin Zephaniah.

Lord Prescott tried to turn the audience against me at some implausible do when New Labour were about to save public transport. There happened to be a bus strike on at the time, and I said so, and he took fat umbrage at that, even though everyone knew that that was why we were all starting half an hour late, with not everybody having two Jaguars.

I've introduced brass bands and choir concerts and declared everybody in the wrong order.

I've been on panels of experts answering questions, and never been asked any.

I've turned up in horribly wrong clothes, and got names and sexes mixed up at serious functions, including funerals.

Nothing however was as bad as Knutty's night in Rotherham, where I am now about to die.

I step onto the dance floor and there's the most godalmighty feedback.

At least one person per table gets up, disappointed that they've had to sacrifice their hearing for charity.

I explain who I am not.

The staff begin to clear, not quietly.

I tell the audience I knew Tony Capstick. I hear a hostile murmur from regular readers of the *Rotherham Advertiser* who remember that I was the one who murdered him.

I tell them it's Bobby Knutt's fault I'm here. The murmuring is angrier, as they realise I am obviously planning to spend my whole forty minute spot slagging off brave local comedians, and no doubt it'll be Paul Shane next.

I tell them how my son Goronwy gathers his crowds in the street by claps and cheers and I ask them to do some now, so that people everywhere else in the hotel will come running in to see what's going on, and we'll double the audience.

That goes down badly. Why should they double my audience for me? With people who haven't paid?

What kind of name is *Goronwy,* anyway? We don't have Goronwys in Rotherham thanks for nowt.

I recognise a bloke I once interviewed, and insist on him volunteering himself onto the dance floor to be my beautiful assistant.

I get applause for him, twice, because we can do better than that can't we? And no we can't. I explain I have seen my Goronwy do this with crowds, finally getting his volunteers to hold his six feet unicycle while he wobbles up on it, to massed applause and money. I deal with a woman heckler who thinks Goronwy should be doing the gig not me if he's so marvellous. My volunteer sneaks back to his table.

More unease. Surely it's time for the disco? Or a smoke? Or Paul Hudson? Or bed?

I tell them I know the funniest joke in the world. This man goes into the *Fleur De Lys* and asks the barmaid for a *double entendre.*[208]

I sense it is a mistake to go into French in Rotherham.

I swerve back into Yorkshire and go for the joke about the man whose wife died.

A widower leaves.

I feed back on godalmighty purpose.

I make a joke about a council leader and his wardrobe. That is also a mistake in Rotherham.

I sense they are now thinking something on the lines of –

> *Who is this bloke in the cheap suit talking about men who's wives die? We can all die. And wardrobes? He should wash his mouth out. And he's probably getting a fatarsed BBC bonus for this. Let's have a Tory government, that'll sort them.*

I go straight into an explanation of the licence fee and note that I have now been speaking for three and a half minutes.

I tell them about Gilly Woods, Maisie, the phone call, the wine, Mike Kay and the Crucible.

I tell them about my wonderful daughters, the last refuge of the scoundrel.

I try the Gordon Brown trick that he used to make sure he lost the election -

> *Look I know you don't like me. I don't like myself much. I am a knobhead, but I'm all you've got.*

I say at least I didn't bring the Autoharp!

A Rotherham Autoharpist takes umbrage in the dark.

I go through the menu to say how much I have enjoyed each course. Two steelworkers go under their table to make their own entertainment.

I praise the table decorations.

---

208 She gives him one.

And the achievement of the evening in general.

And say I will most certainly talk about it on Radio Sheffield. Someone sings old Radio Hallam jingles. Someone always does.

I say they have been my most wonderful audience tonight.

I say that performance itself is a reason for optimism, when people gather together to enjoy themselves, as Clare Venables herself once said. They think I said Terry Venables, and snort.

I try Brecht -

> At last
> The lights go down which shows up the miserable
> Botched job; twilight falls on -

They are alienated.

I tell them if they let me know where they're working next week I'll come and see them! But I say I'll give them a bit of Shakespeare before I go if I can, and I do before they can say I can't.

> I am Cinna the poet! I am not Cinna the conspirator.
> Aaaaaaaaaaaaagh!

I say I hope they've enjoyed me and if they have I'm Paul Shane. If they haven't I've been Bobby Knutt!

I clap them, which is a trick from the alternative theatres of the 80s when you applaud your audience for enjoying the show, and they join in before they can say Jack Robinson and realise they haven't.

I wave to Donna and mime that I need the loo and -

Two minutes later I'm in the foyer giving Reception £5 to get me a £25 taxi, and I hide behind a *Horse and Hound* till it arrives.

*

When Knutty came sunburned back from his cruise he asked how I thought it had gone?

I said I'd died.

He said Donna disagreed. She'd said I'd only been very very poorly.

Ye Olden Days

When Sally and I moved into our little Totley terrace cottage overlooking the park a couple of years ago we didn't have much between us.

Especially cups and saucers.

Now, Michael Dowse has often said on the radio what bargains there are in second-hand crockery, so we went to one of his auctions to buy some.

We didn't buy any.

We bought loads of books instead, in two lots.

The first lot was all Shakespeares and reference.

The other lot was some Pevsners and loads of local stuff including five copies of Mary Walton's *Sheffield History,* a book about Sheffield medicine by Mr Gumpert, and *A History of the Sheffield Repertory Theatre* compiled and written by T. Alec Seed that I didn't know had ever been written or compiled by anyone, let alone by T. Alec Seed, or published in 1959.

I also didn't know something else.

T. Alec Seed's book on the Rep includes *The Little Theatre* at Shipton Street and South Street. It also tells of the Rep-in-exile in Southport, the return to Towhead Street, and the rebuilding of the *Playhouse,* twenty years before the *Crucible.*

I was chuffed, not just to have bought books instead of crockery, but also because my Dad had often talked about these people with the funny theatrical funnynames – the Lillian Meekes, Jenkins Gibsons and Laurie Lingards.[209]

I already knew Dad had had been some part of Shipton Street and South Street theatres, because there was a long lost sepia photo of him with a bloody eye bandage in some Irish play.[210]

---

209 I met him once when he seemed to be hanging about in the Playhouse foyer trying to put people off.
210 Playboy of the Western World. And it turned up while I was researching these memoirs. One of the books I inherited from Lily was her 23-year-old's paperback of WB Yeats' The Countess Cathleen with her looping premarried signature at the front. The terrible last words of that play are - The years like great black oxen tread the world/And God the herdsman goads

And he'd told us how, when he was wallahing at The Town Hall as a young man he used to put an open copy of that month's play in the top drawer of his desk so he could learn his lines, when the City Treasurer wasn't looking.

I flicked through T. Alec Seed's book, and was reminded of my own *Playhouse* days as a kid, watching the first stirrings of documentary theatre with local stories like *Harvey Teasdale* and *Ringa Ringa Roses,* and listening to young John Osborne shrieking at ducks in the lounge. I knew the sweep of those curtains and the greasy sexy smell when you were suddenly taken somewhere else at quarter to eight on a Sheffield evening. I also -

And suddenly, here, look, right at the back of T. Alec Seed's book, page 128, Appendix E, a list of amateur artists who -

> *have given their services to the Sheffield Repertory Company with dates of their first stage appearances*

And look! Here! On page 133 the funnynamed -

> *S. Gethin Robinson 1922*

So in this book of Sheffield theatrical services of Alec Guinness, Patrick McGoohan, Bernard Miles, Peter Sallis, Keith Barron, Anna Wing[211] and Donald Wolfit there is -

> *S. Gethin Robinson 1922!*

No wonder he was so proud of my plays in Sheffield.

(No wonder I am so proud of his.)

*

---

them on behind/And I am broken by their passing feet.
211 Anna Wing was wonderful as Olive Schreiner in my second Edward Carpenter play. Her son Mark Wing-Davey did the music for it, and was DH Lawrence as well. He introduced me to this Ian McEwan bloke who played his flute when he came round our house. Anna in the play was in love with Michael Gough. Michael Gough later named me a genius from the stage of the National Theatre. There's name-dropping for you. All lovely people too. Anna was later the old Mrs Beale in Albert Square. I don't know what happened to Ian McEwan.

He gave his services. And soon enough so did we, and with our own funny names.

Goronwy M. G. Robinson Thom 1986[212]
M. Aphra Robinson Thom 1998[213]
E. R. Robinson Thom 2000[214]
J. Goronwy Robinson 2007[215]

212 A Doll's House, his first paid gig, aged 8. (He read these memoirs, and said he was 4).
213 Opera North opera.
214 Charley.
215 Buttons(!) in a Radio Sheffield panto.

Yesterday's Radio
or
My 6926th Programme[216]

Radio gets forgotten.

Affairs don't stay current.

There's always another one along in a few minutes.

But during my 6926th radio programme, I scribbled notes about what was going, though I shredded most of them by mistake at the end of the programme. I wrote it up straight after, before anything else happened, which is what journalism means.

Episode 6926 isn't typical, except there aren't any typical ones.

6926 also happens to be the first day of the new Lib/Con Coalition, 2010, when Nicolette gave me a photo.

I chose 6926 because this book was nearly finished and I wanted it to have a bit of now in it, as well as a lot of then.

                                        *

I get in at 9.37, a tad late.

Find Rav in his new seat in the newsroom and say what a great programme today's going to be, judging by the e-mail he sent me last night.

He says it's all changed.

I go into the studio to log on, and check the screen for what there is so far.

Has Robin Hood survived from last night's e-mail? Or the mother of the 20-year-old? Or the panel of *Rony's Friends,* who today are a woman who had a post office and an ex-footballer who's lost weight?

---

216 Well, I've done over 26 years on Radio Sheffield, 5 shows a week and often 6. Allowing for holidays and 3 days' illness, that's 26 x 52 x 5 (=6760) plus say 13 x 52 for the extra weekend day (= 676) minus say 26 x 20 (520) for holidays and say 39 (39) for training, awards, funerals, floods, births, first nights, plus 2 more months of 6 days a week (48) since the 26th anniversary. Total 6925.

I pass Howie who says, as always, 'Hello to you,' and looks blonder and younger on his new early shift.

I pass through the Ops room where producers[217] sit on the other side of the nearly-soundproof glass and curse presenters.

Jenny says, 'Nice red shirt.'

Nick in blue doesn't speak.

I log on in Studio 2, and, while the computers fire up, watch Toby through the aquarium glass in Studio 1, in a new checked shirt. As in silent film, he bites his nails, wipes his hand over his bosoms and waves his arms.

I peer through the glass into the newsroom. Helen is delivering tea to Alison. Helen took me into Derbyshire yesterday to look for bees in the snow. Alison and I spent election night together last Thursday.

I watch the telly, and turn us up on the radio.

Dan's voxing in Hallam.

Andy comes in with some CDs and we talk about the election. I'm surprised by some of my colleagues' politics.

Jenny announces a jammed road in Chesterfield.

I pass through the newsroom for the kitchen and breakfast.

Everard looks slyly up. 'You luscious today?'

He's never said that before. Because it's the first day of the new government? Because we had dinner together last week for the first time?

Breakfast of orange juice on *Fruit and Fibre,* probably James Vincent's, but he'll be too busy today.

Katie Galbraith is making teas. We say what a funny day it feels. Gary the Boss comes in. 'Ready to go Katie?' She says yes, but doesn't rush.

---

217 Usually including Katrina Bunker whose Radio Dad I am and who one day, I hope with me, will write the definitive comedy about a local radio station in Sheffield. We collect material every day.

I have a second half bowl of *Fruit and Fibre.* On this new schedule I'll lucky to be able to eat or even drink again.

The 9.45 meeting is cooking as I sidle past. Andy K is taking about the new unemployment figures and the Boss is in shirtsleeves and working glasses, gathering ideas on the whiteboard. The radio output is on loud everywhere, as always.

Rav tells me Scriven's coming on, and we'll probably start with him.

Tom from the telly bustles into the TV cupboard in his big shirt.

With black tea, I line up the studios and take control as Jenny corrects her previous traffic news, which had her jam on the wrong road in Chesterfield. I press the button for the news jingle just too soon, and crash her.

Great start, still nervy after all these years.

I have 18 seconds to say what's going to happen in the show, before the bongs.

I make it up, stop three seconds short and open Everard's fader for the 10 o'clock. Here comes the voice of news. Lovely voice, funny man.

Rav in.

Scriven on the phone - tweeting battle going on with the Labour Party.

Weather pre rec.

Queen *Don't Stop Me Now.* No instrumental, no need to talk.

Rav says we've still got the kick boxer and the woman who ran the post office.

I talk to Scriven off air. He did a bold interview with me a few years ago and I've enjoyed him as an interviewee since. And he danced in the Peace Gardens last summer. But this is now.

Coalitions? Lib Dem betrayals? We have a go.

I give him the last word, and talk to Marie from the University about the media and the election, and why we've seen so few women during it. She doesn't seem as bothered as me.

Traffic.

Percy Sledge.

Computer 1, the visual talkback, freezes.

The newsroom is empty. No news then. Only someone's *Whole Grain Wheats* on the desk, and local hero William Hague rasping unheard on the screen above them.

Sinead blond, black and pink arrives in my studio, clicks, fiddles and leaves giggling. I've never known her not like that.

Rav tells me through my cans to go to Dan in Hallam who says he's out-and-about, which is what we have to say when we are, then does live *vox* interviews with the most intelligent electorate in Britain.

Rony's Friends arrive. The woman from the post office isn't. The ex-footballer losing weight hasn't.

We realise the new Prime Minister is younger than we are. Talk about that.

And the Specials.

Calls and texts galore about the coalition.

The 11 o'clock news, no tea yet.

Franca and Katherine bring news into the Ops Room behind the glass and I try to work out from their body language what kind of news they bring. The glass is soundproof the wrong way.

Beyond them I see Toby with Jamie Campbell in the far end of the News Room. Toby's talking with his hands, pulling at his shirt and his shorts, biting his lip, touching his bosoms, and laughing. Of course he is, Jamie's the funniest person at Radio Sheffield, and that's saying something.

Pete McKee is in Studio 1 through the glass. I try to get him to wave.

And suddenly it's the Weather and here we go round the mulberry bush again.

Into the studio comes Jack Scott billed today as the youngest councillor there ever was, talking grown-up about the coalition. We have a go.

Then Westlife.

Politics Prof from the Uni on the phone. Maybe a Tory split coming?

Calls and texts.

BBC expert in Downing Street is interesting on what Clegg's *Deputy* job might mean.

I watch the telly in the studio as Theresa May gets the Home Secretary's job. I've always fancied her a bit.

Rav says the telly sound feed is on OS 3 in case we have to go to George Osborne.

Doncaster Chamber of Commerce comes on saying good and Barnsley Trade Unions come on saying bad.

Too much adrenalin. This is the seventh day full of soapy politics. Everything's got too fast. Brown only resigned yesterday. Good to be here nice and safe in Studio 2.

Music please and -

Then suddenly - Nicolette Williams through the glass.

A tall, rather beautiful weeping woman.

Rav comes in with her. He's at his most Ravconcerned. She's been waiting on her own for ages on the mezzanine floor with the dodgy coffee machine. Is suddenly on air in 87 seconds.

I try being chirpy, tell her all I will do is ask her story, and if it goes wrong it will be my fault but it never has gone wrong in 26 years and -

Rav reassures her more thoughtfully, and offers tea.

Good, at last. I'll get some.

And we're off.

Your life changed on August 30 2007, Nicolette. What happened?

And after all the politics and fret -

Nicolette tells the story.

An RAF lady officer and an RAF padre came to her door and told her that SAC Christopher Bridge, her 20-year-old son, had died when his Land Rover ran over an explosion device when he was on night patrol in Afghanistan.

What happened?

She tells us, not quite crying.

Then she talks about him alive.

Rav speaks blurred through my cans. I say something blurred on air about how her family must think she's so courageous, to be doing this?

And the tea arrives.

His body came back in a -

> *- massive plane. That was a horrific exhaustive day to watch my son's coffin being carried off the plane and paraded in front of me.The coffin was sealed. His injuries were horrific both externally and internally. That is so hard for me to come to terms with, as I couldn't see him. He was my special son and I wanted to see him no matter what. I was assured with DNA results from the post mortem, his ID TAG, dental records etc that it was my brave son. But that still doesn't help me.*

At the military funeral at Shiregreen, all 150 comrades who were with him attended in full uniform. Taking a week of their holidays. He had a fly-over normally only reserved for high-ranking officers.

She goes to his grave every day.

Music. Thank you.[218]

---

218 I e-mailed Nicolette with my version and her approval. She said thanks and adds, 'I was at a friend's house and had a phone call from my neighbour saying she had heard intruders in my back garden and to come back asap. I did and she told me to come into her house first, as I walked into her living room I saw the R.A.F. lady officer and R.A.F. padre stood there, I instantly knew and went hysterical screaming and jumping up and down, screaming there is

Paulette's trail for the afternoon programme.

Songs, the election, texts, e-mails.

Texts about Nicolette, including one from Les saying she's why the troops should come home. And a poem for her about death from Ted in Chesterfield that I read out.

And in the next hour -

A very young Young Conservative to discuss meritocracy.

Listeners, in pairs. A Lib Dem MEP defends the new politics.

A Rotherham MP calls new coalition leaders white public school toffs.

A man calls the Rotherham MP a hypocrite, and asks where he went to school. I check it out on the web as we broadcast.

No chirrup, no challenge today.

Yesterday I challenged the production team to find me a Clegg and they got me a guitar teacher called Mr Clegg who offered his political views.

The one o'clock news with Kate now, and a quarter of an hour out for me, except for one sentence at six-minutes past trailing the last quarter of an hour.

Cup of tea in the kitchen where Paulette and Steph munch, and I tell them how last night I was spell-checking these memoirs, and had been reading again about the wife-swapping club in Attercliffe Steph and I went to. Steph snorts into her munch, Paulette doesn't believe us.

Back to the Studio for 12 minutes past. Play in the weather. More callers, finishing with three at once, coalitioning, without any need of me. Play the traffic in, hear that the Chesterfield road has been cleared up, whatever road it was, play the traffic out, check Paulette's got control, and start logging off.

---

no God. I was desperately struggling to get into my car to drive to my parents while all around the people in the street were switching on their lights to see what all the commotion was. The officer and padre didn't make any attempt to tell me my special son was dead or just injured. It wasn't until I was at my parents' house sobbing uncontrollable in my mum's arms that my dad had to say to them can you come into the kitchen and please tell him what the situation was? After they left, my dad then had to tell me my worst nightmare that I had already assumed that my brave special son had been blown up in a Land Rover and killed.'

Twenty-eight minutes to two, and that's it.

Rav and Katherine come in for our daily download.

We talk about Nicolette. And a bit about the TV election coverage, all the car chases and the aerial shots last night.

And a bit about me and Theresa May.

But I'm too full of adrenalin to be of much use.

And after Nicolette's story…

*

I shred all my papers - except the photo Nicolette gave me as I leaned over to shake hands at the end of her story, with 28 seconds to the next item.

It's her Christopher smiling in sundried fatigues, holding his big gun half a world away.

And Nicolette's already written on the back, with a kiss and a poem -

Thank you very much for wanting to interview me on your show.

The newsroom is filling up again after lunch.

I take the cups to the kitchen, pick up my bag.

Angela Knight the Sheffield Tory ex-councillor now the banker's rep on earth, is on full screen, silent, smiling.

I hang around for a few minutes, but no one's bothered, and at five to two I go home.

Tomorrow, 6927.

Zed

A 2010 World Premiere never performed before, all done for charity, and yours to act out for free.

NANNY
You've got a boy, Daddy.
DADDY
I'm feeling poorly.
NANNY
Or a girl.
DADDY
I've caught a cold from the doctor.
NANNY
We'd better put you to bed then.
I'll see you in five years time, Mummy.
MISS
Who are you?
ME
Ow.
I'm little John Robinson.
MISS
Little John Robinson what?
ME
Ow.
Little John Robinson, Miss.
MISS
In this school we don't spit, swear, nip, bite, scrawl, lift girls' dresses, trump, get above ourselves, tell stories, think we're clever because we're not clever, imagine, or put coke in snowballs.
But we do sing -
The rich man in his castle
The poor man at his gate
Something something something
Each in his own estate.
ME
This is a picture I am painting of our red brick house on the Laverdene estate with its purple roof, Miss.
MISS
Roofs aren't purple.
ME
Ow. Miss.

MISS
Go to Mr Smellor and ask him to cane your painting hand.
MY JANET
Hello?
ME
Hello. I love you.
MY JANET
I know.
ME
J = J!
MY JANET
We are Janet and John!
ME
I don't know what to do next?
MY JANET
You never will with me.
ME
Hello? I love you instead now Julie.
JULIE
I know.
ME
J = J!
I still don't know what to do next?
JULIE
You never will with me either.
ME
Will girls always be difficult?
JULIE
Until you get some girls of your own.
ME
Why are you kissing me goodbye?
JULIE
You are going to the grammar school and you will not talk to a girl again until it's too late.
HEAD
Robinson!
ME
Ow.
I mean ow sir, sir.
HEAD
You passed the 11 plus even if you did turn over two pages in your exam. So let's see if you can pass muster here.

ME
Ow sir.
HEAD
Latin is a dead language
Dead as dead can be
First it killed the Romans
Now it's killing me.
What do you say to that Robinson?
ME
Three bags full sir, sir.
HEAD
Pro bono.
And *ego* in *loco parentis* hereby give you, in return *inter alia* for a life, gender unease and, *pari passu,* shame about your parents, 14 GCEs, 3 A levels, a prize for Scripture and a *ex parte* souvenir copy of *Kennedy's Eating Primer.* Now go directly *via* Oxford.
ME
Sir.
SCOUT
Don't sir me sir.
I sir you Mr Robinson sir.
These are your rooms, sir and this is the oak for you to sport if you need some privacy sir, but you won't.
You have three windows sir and a long gown in return for a lifetime of celibacy and a hundred pounds sir.
ME
I'm not sure if –
DON
Welcome to jolly old Keble Mr Robinson.
Fancy the Boat Club do yah?
Or perhaps you're a high Anglican? Yah?
Smells and bells. Yah?
Hearty or padre that's yer question yah?
ME
I want to edit the university newspaper and say bum to the Queen.
DON
Then you're a very naughty boy.
But we still like you, yah? We like boys.
And at least you've stayed *intacto* for yer four years.
So have this BA Hons second class, and go off be a schoolteacher yah?
Tempus fugit.
KID
Hello sir?

ME
Who are you?
KID
One of your pupils at your London inner-city comprehensive school Mr Robinson sir.
ME
You're very well-behaved for one of my pupils in a London inner-city comprehensive school?
KID
Only at first sir.
But if you stay long enough, we'll get well-behaved again sir.
ME
Then I will stay for ever.
I will devote my life to you.
We will do plays and write stories and make films and poems and go to the theatre and talk and free-school, de-school, re-school, pre-school -
KID
What about reading and writing and spelling sir?
ME
It's 1968!
KID
What about going on to university like you did, sir?
ME
It's 1968! Call me Rony!
DIRECTOR
Hi Rony, it's 1971 and I want you to leave your comprehensive school and write plays for me.
ME
I don't know how to write plays.
DIRECTOR
Get some paper from WH Smith's, and write the names of who's speaking in the margin on the left.
Let the people speak.
Then edit them by cutting out the first, and then the last three speeches in every scene of your draft and Bob's your Aunty.
ME
But I've no idea what to write about.
DIRECTOR
Use your own life!
What have you done with it so far?
ME
I was a sex education teacher.

DIRECTOR
Fabbo!
ME
But I was 27 before I went all the w-
DIRECTOR
Write it down!
ME
In total, I have had 78 lovers if you count every org-
DIRECTOR
Write it up!
ME
No one'll believe me.
DIRECTOR
They don't have to.
It's art.
ME
Where shall I live?
DIRECTOR
In darkened rooms where men and women shout at night, and only the unreal is true!
In secret places of shared dreams.
From high up in Alhambras and Globes, in Phoenixes and Opera Houses you will watch worlds swirl from your seat high among the Gods.
You must tell the stories of people who dare not tell their own. You must put words in the mouths of the silenced.
Hello who's this?
MOTHER
I am the mother of his three children.
ME
Not yet, please. I've only just started. And who are you?
RADICAL MIDWIFE
I'm your radical midwife.
ME
I'm feeling poorly.
DIRECTOR
Write it up, write it down!
RADICAL MIDWIFE
This time - definitely a boy!
ME
I love him but -
RADICAL MIDWIFE
This is milk that's been expressed so that you can breast-feed him.
It's 1980 and you are about to be soaked by the second wave of feminism I am afraid.

ME

I'm afraid as well.

RADICAL MIDWIFE

So you should be.

Here are two more babies. Both girls.

ME

I love them, all three of them, but -

BBC MANDARIN

Dear boy!

ME

Who are you?

BBC MANDARIN

I am the BBC and I claim you with these hideously white BBC hands, and invite you to join us dear boy!

ME

To do what?

BBC MANDARIN

To speak for three hours every morning for 26 years.

ME

What about?

BBC MANDARIN

Oh we leave that to you, this is the BBC dear.

When you can't think of anything to say pull this lever and your audience can listen to Build Me Up Buttercup by the Foundations instead.

THREE WONDERFUL KIDS

Hello Rony!

ME

Hello who are - ?

THREE WONDERFUL KIDS

We are your three wonderful kids and we are growing up so fast you won't recognise us but you can be proud of us anyway. And pay for things.

ME

You are, I know, I will, I am, I do and I love y-

THERAPIST

Lie down. I'm a therapist.

What are you feeling?

ME

I'm not feeling myself.

THERAPIST

Eh?

ME

It's a joke.

THERAPIST

Jokes? After what you've done?

ME
What have I done?
THERAPIST
Oh it's always other people's fault isn't it?
Unless you're boasting about your wonderful children of course.
Men!
WOMAN
Hello I'm S-
ME
Hello. I'm -
NANNY
We know who you are thank you very much. You're little John Robinson and
I'm Nanny Jessop the midwife.
ME
Have you come to look at my bottom again?
NANNY
I'm dead dear, thank you very much.
But I do hope you realise that you now live five doors up from where I trudged
through the war torn blackout to deliver you?
Only two streets from where you were born? And your attic window looks
over the same park you played in, towards the same fields you saw from your
childhood bedroom window when you lay waiting for sleep, pretending to be
a radio station?
ME
I did!
NANNY
Not done much with your life then have you?
When you were born, I couldn't tell if you were a boy or a girl.
ME
You can tell now Nanny. Look!
NANNY
Put that away at once.
You'll catch pneumonia.
ME
It's only a play Nanny.
NANNY
How dare you say it's only a play to me?
You'll be saying it's only a rehearsal next!
ME
It's getting dark Nanny.
NANNY
Night must fall, come along.
ME
What do you want Nanny?

NANNY
At the risk of telling not showing, I have come to deliver you.
ME
Oh. And oh, Nanny, the lights are fading.
NANNY
That's what often happens at the end of plays, John.
ME
It doesn't make sense Nanny!
NANNY
Destiny is something we invented because we can't stand the fact that
everything that happens is accidental.
ME
At last
The lights go down which shows up the miserable
Botched job; twilight falls on the
Lovely nothingness of the misused stage. In the empty
Still mildly smelly auditorium sits the honest
Playwright, unappeased, and does his best
To remember.
NANNY
Is that your little friend Bertolt Brecht who we've all been waiting for?
ME
Yes. He's -
NANNY
He's not worth waiting for, I know that. I never listen to anyone who alliterates
himself. Come on!
ME
But -
NANNY
But me no buts! When I think of all the money you've made from your silly
plays, and you say silly things like only a play!
Right, follow me, there's the Exit.
ME
But -
NANNY (fading)
If you'd got a proper bottom I'd give it a proper slapping. Mind you I think
you'd rather like that from what I've heard!
ME
Who's been talking?
NANNY
Thinking you're so clever writing your silly memoirs!
ME
We're all historians now, Nanny? We remember only what helps us to half
understand the past. But -

NANNY (fading even more)
Well it's not clever and you're not and they're not and there's no point in starting to be clever now anyway is there? Standing there like Burke's Best! Come along John. It's curtains for you.

Curtain

Z-A
Rony Robinson (John Goronwy Robinson BA Dip Ed D Univ)

Lifetime Achievements
Three children (1m 2f)
Novelist (7) Playwright (127) Songwriter (37) Writer of Memoirs (1)[219]
Full English driving licence (3 cars - Peugeot 205, Nissan Micra and Fiat Punto)
Paid-up Trade Unionist (NUS, NUT, TWU, WGGGB, NUJ)
Broadcaster (26 years without a mistake)
Children's Poet (We've Got a Wah Wah)
Editor (Cherwell)
Top mark North of England GCE Divinity.
Beauty Prize Winner (Prestatyn Holiday Camp, Wales)
Gloops Star for school attendance

*

Employment
BBC Employee after 24 years as a freelance, with 25 days holiday
Resident writer Crucible Theatre (2x), Deptford Green School, and Theatre Royal Stratford East
Head of English (Sedgehill Comp London SE 9)
Supply teacher (Woodthorpe Primary, Sheffield)
Unemployed (9 months)
English teacher (Eltham Green Comp London SE 6)
Labourer for Sheffield City Council City Engineers, Abbey Lane, Sheffield
Clerk in Water Department Sheffield Town Hall
Labourer for Concrete Firm Frazzis, Hillsborough Sheffield
Postal sorter, and postman, GPO Fitzalan Square and Dore Sorting Office

*

Education
Sheffield Hallam University Honorary Doctor, for services to the arts and broadcasting
Oxford Department of Education, Diploma of Education
Keble College Oxford, Open Scholarship and 2nd class BA history degree.
King Edward VII School Sheffield (14 GCE O levels, 3 A levels) Prefect and Captain of Wentworth House.
All Saints, Totley, Derbyshire, Sheffield, Yorkshire, Europe etc

---

219 My Eleanor always calls this book a novel, as if she thinks it's all made up anyway.